PASTORAL CARE
THE CORE OF CHRISTIAN MINISTRY

DAVID B PETTETT

Ark House Press
arkhousepress.com

© 2023 David B Pettett

All rights reserved. Apart from any fair dealing for the purpose of study, research, criticism, or review, as permitted under the Copyright Act, no part may be reproduced by any process without written permission.

Scripture quotations are from The ESV® Bible (The Holy Bible, English Standard Version®), copyright © 2001 by Crossway, a publishing ministry of Good News Publishers. Used by permission. All rights reserved.

Cataloguing in Publication Data:
Title: Pastoral Care: The Core of Christian Ministry
ISBN: 978-0-6456705-7-8 (pbk)
Subjects: REL074000 [RELIGION/Christian Ministry/Pastoral Resources]; REL023000 [RELIGION/Christian Ministry/Discipleship]; REL109000 [RELIGION/Christian Ministry/General]

Design by initiateagency.com

"You hold in your hands a book in which David Pettett has added to the store of works on pastoral care. Unlike some works in this field. which draw on a particular metaphor or historical insight, David's starting point is an examination of core scriptural texts. He writes with the insight of a practitioner of decades and one who has reflected biblically on that practice. He has personally ministered in many contexts at a grassroots level and as a leader of others in various ministries.

In the academic environment David has been 'Pastoral and Church Focused Ministries' Moderator at the Australian College of Theology (ACT) since 2016. The ACT is a consortium of 16 seminaries throughout Australia with a combined student enrolment of around 3,000. David's role involves the oversight of the marking standards in the very fields about which he has written. He is constantly interacting with the teaching of faculty members via the output of their students, but before that in the construction of the courses themselves. His role is to approve the delivery methods and assessments proposed by the various faculty members and then weigh the marking of the faculty.

By observing both the teaching and assessment method and the learning product of the ACT students David has determined there is a great need for a deeper understanding of the integral role of pastoral care in all of a person's ministry. It is this which leads him to focus on the exegesis of Ephesians 4:11 and draw the multiple implications of that verse, in its context, for pastoral ministry.

David's writing style is suited to a well taught lay person or first-time student of theology and thus will form a valuable introduction and a solid biblical basis for later studies and reflection. It will quickly become an appreciated resource within the Australian and other contexts."

Rev Dr Stuart Brooking
Executive Director, Local Leaders International
Head of Ministry and Practice, Australian College of Theology

"I am happy to testify that this book by David Pettett is a much-needed exploration into the biblical basis for pastoral care and its implications for pastoral ministry.

David shines a light into a dark place, into the gap between the position of pastors who may happily but wrongheadedly outsource pastoral care to untrained others in a way that practically devalues its true biblical importance, and that of Christian members of the therapeutic professions who, in practice, may not be referencing foundational biblical truths in their care of others at all, but may in fact be unwittingly beholden to foundational worldviews that are inimical to Scripture itself.

David has served for many decades in pastoral ministry; in parish in Sydney as a rector, as a missionary in Japan through OMF, as a chaplain in a range of roles including naval, hospital and prison, as a manager of chaplains at Anglicare, Sydney, as a lecturer at Moore Theological College in Sydney, and more recently, at Bishop Patteson Theological College, where he is Head of Biblical Studies. David is also currently Moderator of Pastoral and Church Focused Ministries for the Australian College of Theology, a role he has held since 2016.

David Pettett is uniquely equipped to speak to the theological and biblical underpinnings of pastoral care as it relates both to churches, chaplaincy ministries and the helping professions after years of faithful practice in ministry. As such, his book has direct relevance to a broad audience concerned with Christian care."

Rev. Stuart Adamson
Associate Dean
Chaplaincy & Spiritual Care
Morling College, Sydney

CONTENTS

Acknowledgements 9
Introduction 11
    Pastoral Care – Theology Applied to Christian Living 11
    Defining our terms 13
    Getting Sunday Right 22
    Pastoral Care is Biblical 23
    Conclusion 27

1   THE PASTOR TEACHER AND THE CORE OF CHRISTIAN MINISTRY 29
    Discernment 29
    The core of ministry 32
    Equipping the saints 33
    Apostles, Prophets and Evangelists 35
    Pastor Teachers 41
    Building the Body 45
    Conclusion 47

2   THE PASTOR THEOLOGIAN –
    GETTING THE BALANCE RIGHT AND WHY WE DON'T 50
    Theology in Pastoral Care 50
    Why we lose the balance – and how to avoid it 56

  Too much business..60
  Being with people..62
  Pastor Theologian – Equipping the Saints for Life 66
  Avoiding pharisaic obedience..72

3 **WHAT IS PASTORAL CARE?**..77
  Pastoral Care and the Priesthood of all believers............................77
  Equipped to Build the Body..81
  The Pastoral Care Setting 83
  Equipped to Live in the World 84
  Conclusion 96

4 **EXPRESSING THE CHARACTER OF GOD IN PASTORAL CARE.** 98
  God's Fellowship with Humanity..98

5 **GETTING SUNDAY RIGHT**... 116
  What are we supposed to be doing on Sunday? – A Theology of
  Church 116
  The Core of Pastoral Care 117
  What is essential to Sunday.. 121
  Being Christian in the World... 126
  Dealing with Divisions 128
  The Beauty of Sundays... 129
  Sunday is for the Saints... 134
  Conclusion 136

6 **PASTORAL COUNSELLING** 138
  Pastoral Care on the Run... 139
  Triangulation 143
  Process 148

    Emotion 149
    Identifying Emotion... 151
    Discovering Emotional Processes 153
    Being Aware of Our Own Emotions 155
    Listening to God... 157
    Ministering to the Sick 158
    Conclusion 161

7 PASTORAL DISCIPLINE **163**
    Calling Out Ungodly Behaviour.. 163
    Sharply Rebuke 164
    Go to Him 169
    Understanding Forgiveness.. 172
    Accountability.. 178
Conclusion 181
Bibliography... 186

ACKNOWLEDGEMENTS

I am grateful to friends and family who have demonstrated great patience with me as I have tried to put my thoughts for this book onto paper in a way that makes some sort of sense. I have a tendency, when I see others doing things I disagree with, to be somewhat critical. In early drafts some of the incidents I describe in this book of people doing things I believe are less than helpful for the pastoral care and growth of others, were written with a bit of a polemical tone. If I have succeeded in toning down my language it is entirely due to the gracious, patient and irenic advice of my son, Matt. Matt has also challenged me to rethink some of the theological issues I seek to express.

My son, Chris, has also given invaluable advice and feedback on my writing style. With his own writing skills, he has directed me to rephrase, reshape and re-edit. All this has contributed to making the whole book more readable.

My longstanding friend, Raymond Heslehurst, has offered so much advice for this volume it is hard to identify what I have taken from him. We have engaged in so many conversations on theology, doctrine, exegesis, preaching and pastoral care over the years it is impossible to distinguish what, in this book, is an original thought of my own and what I have simply integrated into my thinking through my many discussions with Raymond. Through our undergraduate days to our years of part time Ph.D. research together and beyond, I find I am always wanting to run my latest thinking by Raymond to help me clarify my thoughts. In the present volume I owe him a great debt with regard to the exegesis of Ephesians 4:11 – 12, though I have to say that he disagrees with me about the identity of "evangelists" in v. 11. The title and basic thesis of Chapter Five are entirely Raymond's.

I am also very much indebted to two colleagues with whom I developed a course in pastoral care for Anglicare, Sydney. Kate Bradford and Stuart Adamson very kindly agreed to review the first few chapters. Their input has been invaluable and challenged me to think more deeply and carefully about some of the ideas I am trying to express in this book.

The enthusiasm and encouragement of James Newman and Nicole Danswan at Ark House Press has been inspiring.

I have listened, learned, assessed, accepted and sometimes rejected the advice and thoughts of these friends. And while I have interacted with them and others, the book you hold in your hands is my work, and you should not hold anyone else accountable for errors and thoughts you disagree with. I look forward to robust, respectful discussion about any points in this book you would like clarified or with which you disagree. I welcome any response that will help us develop a better practice of pastoral care. Feel free to email me at davidbpettett@gmail.com

INTRODUCTION

PASTORAL CARE – THEOLOGY APPLIED TO CHRISTIAN LIVING

This book is for pastors. It is about pastoral care and its place in Christian ministry. Pastoral care is an exercise in practical theology applied to Christian living. This book is written specifically for those who are engaged in pastoral ministry or are training for Christian ministry. At the same time, this is a book for those wondering what pastoral ministry is all about. This second group of people is made up of members of a Christian congregation. This is a group of people who may be wondering just what their pastors are up to, or what they should be up to. My aim in writing this book is to give a clear understanding of pastoral care and how it lies at the core of pastoral ministry. I give some real-life illustrations and some practical advice, with a view to pastors integrating pastoral care into their whole ministry.

The major theme of this book is that the work pastors do, is first and foremost about pastoral care. I'll discuss what I mean by *pastoral care* throughout the book but, to give you a taste, Christian pastoral care is based on a rigorous theological foundation and in practice is profoundly theological. My contention then is that Christian pastoral care should not be left to people untrained in theology. I also hope that by the time you have finished reading this book you will be convinced that *pastoral care* is applied to the whole of life and is not limited to providing care in crisis situations.

In his book, *Shepherding God's Flock*, Jay Adams, way back in 1974, made the same point. He said, "it is irresponsible and dangerous to do practical work apart from a sound theological base. The only proper basis for Christian living and pastoral ministry is biblical and theological."[1] I believe this essential base of pastoral care has been lost in the way pastoral care is now practiced in the 21st century. The biblical and theological focus of pastoral care has been overwhelmed by a focus on the human sciences. A further problem with current day practice of pastoral care is that the term seems to be only applied to what is done for people in crisis situations.

Insisting that pastoral ministry is biblical and theological does not mean that people without formal theological training can't be caring Christian people. Of course, they are. Knowing the mercy of God in our lives drives us to have compassion for others. Every Christian will strive to be pastorally caring for others. Christian care should be biblically and theologically based rather than taking its lead from the secular world. We want to care for others because God first cared for us. In the focus of this book, however, I am suggesting that those who believe God wants them to engage in pastoral ministry must have a good theological education undergirding and informing their pastoral practise.

---

1   Jay E Adams. *Shepherding God's Flock: A Handbook on Pastoral Ministry, Counseling, and Leadership.* (Zondervan. Grand Rapids. 1974 1975): 13.

DEFINING OUR TERMS

The term *Pastoral Care* has come to mean many different things. Mostly these different meanings are divorced from what the term originally meant. The basic thesis of this book is that pastoral care has been hijacked, not just the term, but the practice as well. In fact, this hijacking of the practice of pastoral care is my main concern. In a recent article in the Journal of Psychology and Christianity, Chris Leins says, "The functional aim of pastoral counseling now appears to be little more than a merely spiritualized form of psychological practice."[2] I hope that by the time you have finished reading this book you will be as horrified as I am about how pastoral care has so changed from its original intent and meaning that you will work hard to restore pastoral care to its rightful place and meaning in its Christian context, at the core of the work that pastors do.

This book is for pastors. That is, it is a book for people who have a degree in theology who have been recognised or ordained by their church or denomination to lead a congregation of God's people. This book is for you because it is my belief that a great part of the misunderstanding of the nature of pastoral care is the responsibility of pastors. There are so many competing demands in ministry that lacking a rigorous, theological and biblical understanding of the nature of pastoral care has allowed this vital ministry to be relegated outside the core ministry of the pastor teacher.

This book is also for those training for pastoral ministry. It is a book

---

2   Chris J. K. Leins. "What Makes Pastoral Counseling So Pastoral? Distinguishing Between Pastoral Care and Clinical Practice in Modern Life," *Journal of Psychology and Christianity,* Vol. 40, No. 4 (2021): 344-356

for our theological colleges and seminaries. It encourages you to see the whole of Christian ministry as pastoral care. Pastoral care is not something to be tacked on, if we have time, after we have taught theology, church history and doctrine. Pastoral care invades all aspects of theological education. Theological education does not seek to fill heads with knowledge. Theological education seeks to develop men and women who have a deep relationship with God and can apply their understanding of that relationship to help others know God more deeply in the ordinariness of life.

Pastoral care has an essential place in the ministry of the word of God. We have allowed our understanding of the place of pastoral care in ministry to slip out of the core role of the pastor to some extent because we have accepted a secular definition of pastoral care which has narrowed the activity to some functions which are only a part of Christian pastoral care. Because of this narrowing, we have tended to outsource what we now call pastoral care to people who have qualifications in psychology or counselling, believing they are better qualified to understand the human condition than pastors who have been trained in theology. I want to broaden the definition of *pastoral care* to encompass a whole-of-life meaning. More on this later.

There is a great deal we can learn from psychology and other human sciences about the nature of humanity and ways to help people who struggle in life. We can incorporate many of those insights into our pastoral practice. But pastoral care is first and foremost a spiritual discipline and remains firmly in the realm of theology, not psychology.

James and Sylvia, a couple in their mid 80s, were out shopping when Sylvia collapsed and was rushed to hospital. The diagnosis was not good, and James was told he should prepare for the worst. When the chaplain arrived, James, standing by the bed of his unconscious wife, wringing his hands, pleaded with him, "Tell me she's going to be alright." A psychological response to this heartfelt plea would be to encourage James to acknowledge his own distress. The chaplain realised James was not asking whether or not Sylvia would recover. He was aware she was about to die. His question was really, "Will God take care of her?"

There is nothing wrong with the psychological response to James' distress and it would ultimately help him emotionally with Sylvia's sudden death. On the other hand, the chaplain's answer to the theological question James is asking, is the pastoral care James is seeking and a theological answer, that sensitively recognises James' distress, is the core issue of pastoral care.

Pastoral care is the work which focuses on the salvation and sanctification of Christ's flock. Secular counselling and psychology say very little about forgiveness and even less about sin and judgement. There is no thought in these secular disciplines about humanity being created in the image of God. These disciplines therefore have very little to say to the most fundamental issues of human flourishing.

James' question of the chaplain was a fundamental question of human existence based on a theological understanding of Hebrews 9:27 that, "it is appointed for a person to die once, and after that to face judgement." James wanted to know if Sylvia would be O.K. as she faced her judge.

It is sometimes right to refer a member of our congregation to a counsellor but outsourcing *pastoral care* to a counsellor is a fundamental mistake and a misunderstanding of the nature of pastoral ministry and the body of Christ.

It is important to say at this point that there is a place for pastors to engage in pastoral counselling. This is part of their role as pastors. They will therefore need some understanding and skill in the area of counselling. Later in this book we look at some important but basic issues of counselling practice. However, a pastor remains a pastor. Normally a pastor is not a trained counsellor and must therefore be aware when their basic counselling skills are inadequate to help a person. They must be aware of the right time to refer a person for professional counselling.

In this book I have a narrow definition of Christian ministry. It is something the saints do, and its purpose is to build the body of Christ. I therefore refer to the ministry of the ordained person, the priest, minister or pastor of a congregation as, *pastoral ministry* to distinguish it from what the saints do. I also have a narrow definition of *the body of Christ*. It is the local congregation. We often hear that "our church" is part of the body of Christ, meaning, our local congregation is a part of the church universal, or it is part of the sum total of all Christians throughout the world. I think, however, the New Testament leads us to understand that the local congregation is the complete body of Christ in that, a local church has within it every aspect of the body of Christ. Each local church is not part of the body but, rather, is the body of Christ. More on this later.

Because the purpose of what the pastor teacher does, along with the ministries of apostles, prophets and evangelists, is to equip the saints to build the body of Christ, pastoral care goes beyond what some people call *mercy ministries*. These are usually thought to be things like providing food for the hungry, clothing, housing, counselling etc. Mercy ministries are a very small part of pastoral care which focuses on equipping the saints so that the body of Christ is built into unity and maturity. Pastoral care is much more of a whole person ministry than the limits of providing for a person's material needs. I am not saying these are wrong things to do. I think they are essential things for Christians to be engaged in. They reflect God's love and compassion. I would love to see more congregations involved in these types of ministries. But here, I am trying to define my terms in the light of what the New Testament says about Christian ministry and pastoral care. I am trying to do this because I think we have not been rigorous enough in our definitions and pastoral care has been hijacked by secular ideas and definitions. Inevitably these secular ideas lead us away from doing Christian ministry and Christian pastoral care in ways the New Testament tells us we should be doing them.

There is an old term that describes the essence of the role of a person ordained to pastoral ministry. That term is, *Cure of Souls*. It simply means caring for people with a fundamental understanding that they are *souls*. That is, they are human beings who have a spiritual dimension. This spiritual dimension is essential to the essence of who we are as human beings. Understood from a Christian perspective, this spiritual dimension in the human condition is that all people are created in the image of God. The *cure of souls* is the fundamental focus of pastoral ministry. Whatever a Christian pastor is doing, if he or she does not have the cure of souls as the primary motivation for everything they are doing, they are not engaging in pastoral ministry.

As the term *pastoral care* has shifted in meaning in the modern world, so also has the understanding of the word *spiritual* changed meaning. *Spiritual* has come to mean something that gives a person meaning in life. If you have an experience you believe touches your inner being, your soul, in the modern context this is spoken of as a spiritual experience. This definition of *spiritual* is a far cry from a Christian understanding of the word. Jesus explained to the Samaritan woman at the well that God seeks people who worship him in spirit and in truth (John 4:24). In context, the Spirit Jesus talks about is the Holy Spirit himself. We cannot truly worship God without the movement of the Holy Spirit within us. We cannot say, "Jesus is Lord" except by the Holy Spirit (see 1 Corinthians 12:3) and if we do not have the Spirit we do not belong to Christ (Romans 8:9). Christian pastoral care therefore cannot seriously leave a person in need believing that they have spiritual understanding or growth if they do not have the Holy Spirit. Leaving pastoral care in the hands of a psychologist or counsellor who doesn't have a clear theological understanding of the role of the Holy Spirit in a person's life is, for the Christian pastor, to abdicate their office and obligation to be the person who has responsibility for the cure of souls.

I am not advocating for Christian pastors to become counsellors or psychologists. As pastoral care is an exercise of practical theology Christian pastoral care is the responsibility, first and foremost, of the pastor who has responsibility for the cure of souls. This responsibility is exercised primarily in a theological framework. What can be learned from the human sciences will be very helpful, but these learnings will also be subject to a biblical and theological framework. The Christian pastor will continue in their responsibility to teach the Scriptures, to drive away all heresy and false doctrine, to seek out the lost and to care for God's flock as an under-shepherd. All these activities are best done with a clear understanding that in all of them you are exercising pastoral care.

Pastoral care should not be seen as something done apart from what the pastor does. In other words, the pastor does not outsource pastoral care. Every aspect of the pastor's ministry is pastoral care. I fill out this idea in Chapter Five, "Getting Sunday Right."

INTRODUCTION

Some clergy see their gifts to be in the area of preaching and teaching. This idea comes from Ephesians 4:11 where Paul says that when he ascended Christ gave apostles, prophets, evangelists, pastors and teachers. These ministries are the one gift[3] of Christ to the church. The role of the clergy is seen to be that of pastor/teacher and that means preaching and teaching. I have no problem with this idea except when it is limited to a role of just preaching/teaching and pastoral care is thought to be best left to others who are trained in counselling or psychology. I am also concerned if pastors mean their pastoral care is done only in their preaching. The aim of this book is to convince you that everything the pastor does is pastoral care. At the same time, when you have finished reading this book, I want you to be convinced that pastoral care is done in preaching and teaching. In fact, I want you to be convinced that preaching and teaching that does not have pastoral care as its primary focus is not Christian preaching and teaching at all. The whole goal of preaching and teaching is to pastorally care for God's people. But preaching alone is only one arrow in the pastor's quiver of pastoral care. Everything the pastor teacher does must have pastoral care as its primary focus.

The idea that every aspect of the pastor's ministry is pastoral care, falls foul of modern thinking about pastoral care. But this modern thinking has abandoned a proper understanding of Christian pastoral care. If the preaching and teaching of Christian pastors does not pastorally care for those for whom they have the cure of souls, we should question if this is true Christian preaching and teaching. I agree with those who tell their

---

3   The singular is deliberate. For reasons I'll explain in Chapter One, I believe that 'apostles, prophets, evangelists, pastor/teachers' are one gift to God's people. These four ministries are one package, one gift from God to each of us. And, yes, I mean four. I see "pastors and teachers" as the one ministry. I also explain this is Chapter One.

congregation to come to church every Sunday so they hear the preaching because this is where the pastor does their pastoral care. A sermon that shows no pastoral care for the people listening is no sermon at all. At the same time, the sermon should not be the only place a pastor does pastoral care. There are many aspects to the privilege of pastoral ministry which we will be touching on throughout this book. A well-rounded pastor who has the cure of souls is more than a great preacher. Inevitably they will find themselves caring for people in crisis situations. A well-rounded pastor will need some counselling skills. Chapter Six gives an introduction to some of those skills.

A pastor who sees their role in terms of Ephesians 4:11 as being a *pastor teacher* will recognise this gift of God to His church is a gift which equips God's people, the saints, for the work of ministry, for the building of the body of Christ (Ephesians 4:12). To equip the saints to build the body of Christ requires the pastor to do a whole lot more than preach, expecting members of the church to turn up every Sunday. The pastor will leave the study and be out where the people of God live and work and have their daily interactions. The pastor will interact with God's people, learning from them about their daily concerns, helping them to live as God's people in the world and bringing care to those in need. Balance is needed. Time in the study and time in the world, the world the saints live in each week, all with a view to equipping the saints. All with a view to build the body of Christ. This is pastoral care.

Our modern world sees pastoral care as something you do for people who are in crisis. Our theological colleges and seminaries do not help. They offer courses in pastoral care where students are asked to:

Outline a scenario in which a person is seeking pastoral care support in response to:

- Unemployment and work-related stress
- Long term illness e.g. cancer
- Alcoholism or drug dependence
- Domestic violence or abuse

Some of our theological colleges are teaching that pastoral care is for people who are in a crisis situation in which they need help. These colleges are teaching that people who are sick need pastoral care. People who are having difficulties in a relationship need pastoral care. People with mental illness need pastoral care. People who are dying need pastoral care. While, of course, people in these situations need pastoral care, to limit pastoral care to people in these situations is a very truncated view of pastoral care. Christian pastoral care is so much more, so much richer, so much all-of-life-equipping. Christian pastoral care helps a person to know Jesus and to live a full life under His lordship.

In the 4th century Gregory of Nazianzus said pastoral care is, "to provide the soul with wings, to rescue it from the world and give it to God, and to watch over that which is in His image".[4] Pastoral care is about rescuing a person from the world and giving them to God. It is not about helping a person cope with the world. It is about helping a person who is not of this world to live in it with a focus on God.

There is some complaint in churches today that our theological colleges and seminaries are too academic and don't teach enough pastoral subjects. While I would certainly like to see more teaching on pastoral care

---

4 Quoted in Andrew Purves, *Pastoral Theology in the Classical Tradition* p.9

in our seminaries, the academic teaching is not meant to equip people to regurgitate a theological treatise as an excuse for their Sunday sermon. Seminaries exist to equip future pastors, as under-shepherds, to tend the sheep of Jesus. A pastor is trained to think theologically about daily life. His or her pastoral task is to pass on this ability to God's people, whether this be from the Sunday pulpit or one to one in a crisis situation. The task of the pastor is to take what they have learned in seminary and translate it into theology for daily living.

The task of the pastor is to think theologically about the world and to so pastorally care for Christ's sheep that they are equipped to live Christ honouring lives in all aspects of their daily lives in the world. God's people want to be equipped for the work of ministry. They want to be equipped to bring a Christian voice to the public square which they inhabit daily, whether it be in the home, at work, at the football game or at the dinner party. Pastoral care is equipping God's people for these works of ministry.

GETTING SUNDAY RIGHT

One problem I have often heard from the saints is that Sunday does not equip them for the work they want to do, neither in the church nor in the world. Sunday is the most important time for God's people. A time to meet with God's people gathered around the word of God, present with us in the person of Jesus, and present by being both read and proclaimed from the Bible. Gathered as the church of God is a time gathered together with the angels and Archangels and all God's people to sing His praises. A time to bring our communal desires before Him in prayer. A time to give a full and visible expression on earth of the gathering in heaven (Heb. 12:22-24). The people of God are saying to their pastors, "Please get Sunday right." Getting Sunday right is a major aspect of pastoral care.

What the people of God are asking of their pastors when they ask them to "get Sunday right" is to equip them to build the body of Christ and to live Christianly in the world. They not only want to come to church and honour God and feel uplifted. They also want to go into the world prepared to think Christianly about their daily activities. They want to develop a sense of confidence that this Christian life is worth living. Getting Sunday right is real pastoral care because it equips God's people to live in the world. It helps husbands and wives to truly reflect the relationship between Christ and his church in their own marriages (Ephesians 5:25-33). It helps fathers not to exasperate their children but to bring them up in the love and discipline of the Lord (Ephesians 6:4). Getting Sunday right helps children to honour their parents (Ephesians 6:1 – 3). It helps Christian bosses to treat their workers fairly and with Christian grace (Ephesians 6:9). It helps workers to work as though serving the Lord and not as people-pleasers (Ephesians 6:6 - 8). It helps men, women and children to engage with the world in a godly manner so that they bring a Christian influence into the world rather than take on the world's values. Getting Sunday right helps the Christian doctor to be a *Christian* doctor, a Christian builder to be a *Christian* builder, a Christian truck driver to be a *Christian* truck driver.

PASTORAL CARE IS BIBLICAL

In this book I am attempting to understand what the Bible says about ministry and pastoral care. This is because I want to understand God's idea of pastoral care, not the world's idea. I want to understand what the Bible says about pastoral care also because I believe pastoral care must be biblically based. As I said earlier, pastoral care is profoundly theological. You can't be a pastor without being a theologian. It is also true that you can't be a theologian without being a pastor. This is why I have included a chapter on the *Pastor Theologian*. As a *pastor teacher*, what else do you teach other than theology? The pastor teacher must have complete confidence in the Scriptures if we are going to bring the comfort and encouragement of the Lord to His people. All Scripture teaches us about Jesus (Luke 24:27). If we are to introduce people to Jesus and encourage them to grow in him, we must know the Scriptures. We must be the *Pastor Theologian*.

I believe the Bible is the word of God. It is His inerrant infallible word to us. I am not a fundamentalist in the sense that I believe in a six-day creation of literal 24 hours each. How could I believe that when the sun, by which we mark the hours of the day, was not created until the fourth day? The Bible is not a scientific textbook which teaches *how* things happen.[5] The Bible is God speaking to us to tell us *why* things have happened. The fact that Genesis One and Two contain two very different accounts of Creation should alert us to the fact that we are not dealing with science here. The Scriptures teach us who God is, what He has done for us and who He wants us to be.

I believe the events of Jesus' life are historical events. Jesus walked on water. Jesus calmed a storm. These are not the feelings of the disciples whose experience of the person of Jesus caused them to poetically imagine it was just as though he walked on water. It was just as though the

---

5   The exception to this in Genesis Chapter One is that God created the world by His Word. But the point remains. Genesis is not trying to give a scientific account. We shouldn't treat it as if it were.

wind and the waves were stilled by his calming presence. These are not the way the accounts are written. They are written as actual events. That is the way we are meant to read them.

In the boat, on a storm-tossed sea, experienced fishermen were in fear of their lives. It was not that Jesus' calm demeaner inspired the disciples to be calm in the midst of a raging storm. This incident in the life of Jesus is not in the text of Scripture to point us to a universal trait of calmness in the midst of fear. Liberal theologians, who have pointed us in such direction have pointed us away from Christ. The Bible does not include a record of Jesus' miracles to point us to universal ideals. The miracles are there to point us to Jesus. In fact, every word in the Bible is there to point us to Jesus. Theology or pastoral care that does not point us to Jesus is not Christian theology or Christian pastoral care.

We note that the disciples were more afraid *after* Jesus calmed the storm (see Mark 4:35 – 41). These are historical events that teach us a great deal about the person of Jesus. And while they are historical events, they are more than history. The events are recounted to us as the word of God who, by explaining the *meaning* of the events, points us to the Son who gives life.

While we understand the Bible is a record of historical events, we also understand that the events of themselves tell us very little. Jesus was a historical figure. He is not a myth. He is a real person. He was actually born in Bethlehem, grew up in Nazareth, taught with amazing authority, performed some staggering miracles, was crucified, was raised from the dead and ascended into heaven. All of these are historical events, testified to by people who were there at the time and witnessed those events.

More importantly, what these events mean for humanity is what we pay attention to. Those historical events, of themselves, are just that, historical events. The reason they have meaning beyond the simple fact that they happened, is because God has spoken about these events. God has explained them and given them meaning beyond the event itself. Take the crucifixion for example. During the 1st century hundreds, if not thousands of people died by crucifixion. The Romans used this method of capital punishment extensively. At one point the roads of Galilee were lined with tens of people being executed by crucifixion.

In such an historical setting what is it that makes the death of Jesus of Nazareth by crucifixion stand out? Why do we believe that this one death, among the thousands, is our atoning sacrifice? The answer is simply that God says it is. God has spoken to us about this one death and given it meaning beyond all the others. God has said this death has paid the price for our sins. This is the nature of the Bible. It records God's works in history and it gives us God's interpretation of those historical events.

All Scripture is breathed out by God and profitable for teaching, for reproof, for correction, and for training in righteousness, that the man of God may be complete, equipped for every good work (2 Timothy 3:16. ESV). However, there are some things in them that are hard to understand, which the ignorant and unstable twist to their own destruction (2 Peter 3:16. ESV). This is where the role of the pastor teacher comes in. Pastor teachers have the incredibly privileged task of faithfully teaching the Scriptures to God's people. It is a rigorous discipline that requires hard work, but the rigor is done with a Christ inspired compassionate heart towards God's people.

CONCLUSION

Throughout this book I illustrate some of the issues and ideas I am communicating with you by the use of stories. Most of these stories are not fictional. They are the stories of real live people I have encountered over my years of ministry, or they are stories of real life I have heard from others, or they are stories that are in the public domain. In each and every story I tell you in this book I have not used people's names. Where I have used names, I have changed them so that the person is not identified. In some stories I have not used names at all. But most of the stories are real. In some I have attempted to change the details so that the events also are not identifiable. Where the events of a story may be identifiable to some, I have attempted to keep the details as generic as possible to simply aid the teaching of the point I am trying to make.

I grew up and have exercised most of my ministry within an evangelical Anglican context. My thoughts and comments in this book inevitably reflect that background but I hope that you will be able to translate what I am saying about pastoral care into your own context if you have a different Christian denominational experience. I am also an Australian. I hope you will understand my accent and cultural background and be able to also translate this into your own culture. I do, however, have some cross-cultural experience in Japan, where I ministered in the mid 1980s, church planting, and in Solomon Islands, where I currently teach pastoral care and biblical subjects to ordained Anglicans in their theological college.

Modern practice has narrowed the definition of pastoral care to either *mercy ministries* or to pastoral counselling. By the time you have finished reading this book I hope you will agree with me that pastoral care is a whole-of-life ministry of a pastor/teacher who, being trained theologically, has the *cure of souls*.

1

THE PASTOR TEACHER AND THE CORE OF CHRISTIAN MINISTRY

DISCERNMENT

James 3:1 tells us that not many of us should become teachers. The reason James tells us this is because teachers will be judged with "greater strictness". The desire to be a pastor teacher in the church of God is a noble desire but one we must think very carefully about. It is not a role to take on because of any perceived benefits it might give. It is not about prestige or power. There are some very sad examples in recent years of impressive ministries which came tumbling down because of the abuse of power. The only reason to start thinking about becoming a pastor is because this is a role God wants you to take on. Very clear discernment is needed to understand if this is in fact something God wants for you. This discernment cannot be done in isolation.

When a person begins to believe that God wants them to be a pastor in His church the first thing to do is pray, asking God for discernment and wisdom. The next thing to do is ask others to pray for you and with you as you seek to discern God's will. If you are married, your spouse is the first person to discuss this with. Part of the process will be to speak to your own pastor, seeking their wisdom, advice, counsel and prayers. Through all of this you should be reading what the Bible says about the qualifications of overseers and deacons in 1 Tim. 3:1-13. Paul's instructions throughout his two letters to Timothy and his one to Titus should also inform your thinking about the responsibilities of a person who seeks to lead the church of God.

A young friend of mine told his father he thought God wanted him in ordained ministry. His father asked if he was sure this is what he wanted to do. My friend responded that it was not about what he wanted to do. It was a calling. While I have some issues with the idea of a "calling" to ministry (we have one calling in life and that is to follow the Lord Jesus), the point is that my friend recognised his desire was something from God. He had no thought that ministry would give him power or prestige. It was simply something God wanted him to do. He went through a full process of discernment and is now exercising a ministry through which God is blessing many people.

A measure of whether or not you believe God wants you to be a pastor is your attitude to money. It is surprising how closely something seemingly so unrelated can be a measure of spiritual things. This is, of course, one of the issues the apostle Paul points to in his list of the qualifications of a Christian minister. A minister must not be a "lover of money" (1 Timothy 3:3). Love for God must be above love of money.

As I have observed over many years people discerning God's direction for their lives and whether or not that involves full-time Christian ministry,

I have come across one or two who have given themselves a backup plan. Just in case it doesn't work out they make sure they have a second career which they can fall back on. While this seems a commendable thing to do in terms of making sure one's family is provided for it's the wrong approach to ministry. Ministry is not a career. Either God wants you in full-time ministry or He doesn't. If He does, He'll provide for you and your family. If He doesn't want you in pastoral ministry, He'll provide for you and your family. My personal approach is that if you are uncertain that God will provide for you, that is probably a good sign God doesn't want you in ministry. My point is that if you find yourself worrying more about money than equipping yourself to be a pastor, you should probably question if God really wants you in ministry.

Having said that, the most important consideration in discerning whether or not God wants you in ministry is what the scriptures say. Do the passages in Paul about the qualifications of deacons and overseers describe you? There are some qualifications which you may not have at the moment but that which you'll be able to develop, particularly through theological education. There are other qualifications which describe personality traits. These may describe you, or they may not. Some things you can change, some things you cannot. The point is, you should have these qualifications constantly before you and you should be constantly assessing yourself against them. Be honest with yourself before God.

When we are discerning whether or not God wants us in pastoral ministry, we have to be clear on what we think pastoral ministry is. As I've indicated in the Introduction, pastoral ministry is first and foremost, the *cure of souls*.

THE CORE OF MINISTRY

A few months ago, I posted a quote from the introduction of this book on Facebook. I was surprised by some of the responses the post received. The quote was, "Outsourcing pastoral care to a counsellor is a fundamental mistake and misunderstanding of the nature of Christian ministry." One response I received was, "While I agree, just to clarify I assume you mean pastoral care in general and not actual mental health." The response seems to imply there is some sort of priority for mental health when we speak of pastoral care. This illustrates the point that we have lost a clear understanding of what pastoral care is. Modern definitions have narrowed the practise of pastoral care to a point where they now exclude the fundamental meaning of Christian ministry.

Another response I received on the Facebook post was, "Surely it depends on a person's gifts?" In one sense I don't think it depends on a person's gifts at all. What I'm arguing for is that pastoral ministry is fundamental to ordained ministry. Certainly, in the Anglican context (of which I am a part) we are ordained to the *cure of souls*. So, in that sense the person who is not gifted in the cure of souls is not gifted for ministry. A minister who doesn't have a pastoral focus is not doing what they were ordained to do. I don't mean pastors should be trying to take over roles of people who are alcohol and other drugs counsellors or mental health workers for example. What I do mean is that ministry begins with pastoral care. If ministers are doing pastoral care properly (in their preaching for example) there will be less need to find help for people in crisis situations. Proper pastoral care will be equipping the saints for the work of ministry. Now, let's tease out that thought.

EQUIPPING THE SAINTS

In Ephesians 4:11 Paul lists a number of people Christ has given. They are apostles, prophets, evangelists, pastors and teachers. In 4:7 Paul speaks of grace that has been given to each of us according to the measure of the gift of Christ. This gift is Christ. Paul describes the measure of the gift of Christ with superlatives. Christ, who is incarnate ("he who descended", v.10), ascended far above the heavens, that he might fill all things. This measure of the gift of Christ is that he fills all things. In the abundance of the gift of Christ, in the abundance of Christ himself, he has given apostles, prophets, evangelists, pastors and teachers (4:11).[6] When Paul says in 4:7 that grace has been given to each of us according to the measure of the gift of Christ, that measure is beyond measure. That measure is Christ Himself who is incarnate, who ascended far above the heavens, who fills all things.

The grace beyond measure that has been given to each of us is the people listed in verse 11. The grace we have received is apostles, prophets, evangelists, pastors and teachers, and the ministries they exercise. The focus of the verse is on the collective. The different ministries listed are the one act of grace of Christ to each of us. Paul is saying that each of us, every single Christian, has been given apostles, prophets, evangelists, pastors and teachers. It's like receiving a present that when we open it, we discover several items in it. There may be a salad bowl, a coffee pot, a dinner set and a couple of candle sticks. Now, there's a nice gift for someone setting up a home (at least I think so), but it is one gift that contains several items. In this sense Paul is talking about the one act of grace of

---

6   My thinking here has been shaped by a discussion on Academia.com with F. A. Talbot.

Christ being apostles, prophets, evangelists, pastors and teachers. One gift with several items in it.

The fact that Christ has given each us apostles, prophets, evangelists, pastors and teachers does not mean that we are all apostles etc. It simply means that apostles, prophets, evangelists, pastors and teachers have been given to us. In the same way that the gift of a salad bowl to you when setting up a home does not make you a salad bowl, the gift of apostles etc. to you does not make you an apostle. The salad bowl equips you to serve salads to your family and to your friends. The gift of apostles etc. equips you to do ministry in building the body of Christ. In other words, we benefit from the ministry of the apostles. Every Christian benefits from the gift of Christ. The fact that there are apostles in the church is because of Christ's grace to each of us. The fact that there are pastors and teachers in the church, is because of Christ's grace to each of us. The reality may be that some of us are not any of these people at all. That doesn't matter because the purpose of these ministries, this one gracious act of Christ, is to equip all God's people for the work of ministry, to build the body of Christ (the local congregation) to maturity. This work of ministry is the building of the body of Christ. We all will have other gifts, but we are not all apostles, we are not all prophets, we are not all evangelists, and we are not all pastor/teachers (see 1 Corinthians 12:29 – 30).

If you are concerned about what your gift (or gifts) might be (as I have seen many people worry over the years), don't be concerned. You already have your gift. Your gift is Christ who has given, according to his immeasurable measure, apostles, prophets, evangelists, pastors and teachers. You may not be any one of these particular people but together they have been given to you by Christ. The reason Jesus has been so gracious to you is to equip you for works of ministry. So, don't worry about what gift you might have. You already have it. Christ is your gift, and He has given apostles, prophets, evangelists, pastors and teachers. So, knowing what gift you have, get on with the work of ministry to build the body of Christ. You are being equipped for ministry by the gift of Christ to you.

APOSTLES, PROPHETS AND EVANGELISTS

Firstly, I need to say a word about apostles and prophets. Some denominations teach that the ministry of apostles and prophets continues today in real live people. Let me speak about apostles first. While I believe the ministry of the apostles continues today, I disagree with the idea that we can point to real people, alive today, who exercise the ministry of apostles as Paul had it mind in Ephesians 4:11. I especially disagree with this idea because the New Testament teaches that apostles required specific qualifications which it is not possible for a person who did not live in the first century to hold.

When the apostle Peter addressed the brothers after Jesus had ascended, he declared that another person should replace Judas among the twelve. Peter set out the qualifications and the purpose of such a person. In Acts 1:21 – 22 Peter says, "So one of the men who have accompanied us during all the time that the Lord Jesus went in and out among us, beginning from the baptism of John until the day when he was taken up from us—one of these men must become with us a witness to his resurrection." (ESV).

The person required to be an apostle must have been with the group from the beginning, from the baptism of John. This person must have been with them right up to the ascension. They will become, with the other eleven, a witness to the resurrection. This purpose statement has a double meaning. It implies that the person must have seen the risen Jesus, which he would have done if he had been with the group from the day of John's baptism up to the day of the ascension. Being a witness to Jesus' resurrection also points to what the apostles will do. They will be witnesses to the world, that Jesus has been raised from the dead. In this sense, the word "witness" becomes a technical term referring to the work or ministry which the apostles do. It is not possible for a person who was born later than the first century to fulfill these qualifications. It is not possible for a person who was born later than the first century to be an apostle.

Amongst the group on that day there were two men who had the necessary qualifications. They were Justus and Matthias. The lot fell to Matthias, and he became one of the twelve. Note that both Justus and Matthias had the necessary qualifications to become an apostle. But only Matthias was chosen to be a *witness* – someone who had been from the beginning, now appointed to witness to the world that Jesus had been raised from the dead. Justus was not chosen for this task. Even though he had the qualifications, Justus was not chosen to be an apostle. It seems hardly likely then, that any person today could be called *apostle* in the same way those of the first century were.

The apostle Paul received his apostleship in exceptional circumstances. The risen Jesus appeared to him and commissioned him to be His witness to the Gentiles (Acts 9:15).[7] It is these thirteen who have the ministry of

---

[7] Those, "who are of note among the apostles" (Romans 16:7) means, "those who are well known by the apostles" not, "noteworthy apostles". In other words, Andronicus and Junia (mentioned in this verse), were not apostles, but were simply well known by the apostles.

apostle and are referred to by Paul in Ephesians 4:11 as forming part of the gift of Christ to the church to equip the saints for the work of ministry. No one else possesses these unique qualifications.[8] We continue to benefit from the ministry of the apostles today because we have their ministry written down. These words of the apostles in the gospels and letters of the New Testament are part of the gift of God to us to equip us for the work of ministry. It is in this sense that the gift of apostle continues today.

I guess you can give anyone the title of "apostle" if you like. But if you are referring to a living person in your church be aware that you are not using that title the way the New Testament does and that the person you call "apostle" is not like one of the thirteen who were witnesses to the world of the resurrection of Jesus. Those men have all died but their ministry lives on today in the writings they have left us.

This same argument applies to the ministry of prophets. The ministry of the prophets was a very specific ministry where the prophet spoke the words of God to God's people. The essence of biblical prophecy is that the prophet says to God's people, "Thus says the Lord."[9] Prophecy is

---

8   We also note that in Galatians 1:19 Paul refers to James, the Lord's brother, as an apostle. James' unique status as the Lord's brother, and now, "servant of God and of Christ Jesus" (James 1:1) would qualify him (and his brother Jude for that matter) to be called an apostle. In Acts 14:14 Luke identifies Barnabas, on his mission trip with Paul, as an apostle. It seems here that Luke is using the word 'apostle' in the sense of 'sent one' as does Paul in Philippians 2:25 referring to Epaphroditus and in 2 Corinthians 8:3 referring to a group of people. It would be a long stretch of exegetical contortion to include any of these people with that group who were "witness[es] to the resurrection" (Acts 1:22).

9   It is not my intention here to explain this biblical understanding of Prophecy. To do so requires another book. So, I simply refer you to a good Bible dictionary, such as the New Bible Dictionary and its article on *Prophecy, Prophets* by J.A.Motyer for an introductory discussion on the nature of biblical prophecy.

not about foretelling the future, although it often did that. Prophecy is a reminder to God's people of who God is. Prophecy is a call to God's disobedient people to remember God's love to them, to remember the covenant God established with His Son (firstly, His Son, the people of Israel). Prophecy is a call to covenant obedience lest God bring punishment on His disobedient people. Our churches today continue to benefit from the ministry of the prophets because, like the apostles, we have their words written down. These words equip us for the work of ministry.

The New Testament indicates there are people in the churches with the gift of prophecy. This gift seems to be of a different order to the prophecies we have in our Bible. In Acts 21:9 we hear of Philip's four daughters who prophesied but we are not told what they said. In Acts 21:10 – 11 a prophet named Agabus took the apostle Paul's belt and bound his own feet and hands and said, "Thus says the Holy Spirit, 'This is how the Jews at Jerusalem will bind the man who owns this belt and deliver him into the hands of the Gentiles.'"

Agabus' prophecy was of a different nature to the biblical prophets. This prophecy has a clear warning of the future, but not of judgment on a disobedient people who are not living in covenantal faithfulness. Yet it does come within the essence of prophecy in that Agabus declares, "Thus says the Holy Spirit", which in Trinitarian theology has the same meaning as, "Thus says the Lord." What we read of Agabus' prophecy is descriptive and it would therefore be mistaken to take this activity as one which continues today.

In 1 Corinthians 14:1 Paul encourages us to earnestly desire the spiritual gifts, especially that we may prophesy. This gift of prophecy is a gift that speaks to people for their upbuilding and encouragement and consolation and builds up the church (see 1 Corinthians 14:3 – 4). This gift is simply one where a person speaks to upbuild, encourage, console and build up the church. This is the very thing Paul says in Ephesians 4:11 is the purpose of the gift of Christ to his people.

I am all for prophecy being exercised in our churches today. The place I see it operating primarily is in the Scriptures. I have every confidence that when I read the prophets whose words are recorded in the Bible, I am reading words that will equip me for ministry. I do not have the same level of confidence in regard to those who speak today claiming they have a prophecy. I have seen too many false claims of this sacred gift, so I'll stick with the scriptures. But I will also listen carefully to people in my church who speak to me for upbuilding, encouragement and consolation.[10]

Now, with regard to the evangelists mentioned in the list of Christ's gift I want to suggest the thought that Paul is referring to the writers of the first four books of the New Testament when he includes this word in Ephesians 4:11. This is not a common interpretation of this usage, so allow me to defend it.

Throughout Christian history, Matthew, Mark, Luke and John have been known as the evangelists. They wrote of the *evangel*, the good news of Jesus

---

10   I have had friends tell me the Lord has laid on their hearts a word for me. Whether this is a *word of knowledge* or a *prophecy* neither my friend nor I am certain, but I am greatly encouraged by these moments. More often than not, they have been words that have applied to my situation. They show that God is active and that my friend has a particular desire for my good. These words of encouragement are great moments, and they may well fall into the category of prophecy Paul describes in 1 Corinthians 14. So, if you have this gift of encouragement, please keep it up. If you don't have this gift, earnestly desire it.

Christ (see Mark 1:1 for example).[11] Paul certainly knew Mark and Luke personally and is also most likely to have known Matthew and John as well. Matthew, Mark and Luke probably wrote their Gospels in the early A.D. 60s, about the same time Paul wrote to the Ephesians. It is likely, therefore, that Paul knew of these three Gospels and simply meant the Gospel writers when he referred to evangelists in his list in Ephesians 4:11.

Of course, the apostle Paul wants to see the work of evangelism done and people won to Christ. This is part of the thrust of his teaching in 1 Corinthians 14 for example. When Paul speaks throughout his letters about the message of the gospel, he clearly means that he wants to see the good news of Jesus proclaimed so that people come to know Jesus as Lord. But the only time Paul uses the word *evangelist* is in the list in Ephesians 4:11 and in his instruction to Timothy to do the work of an evangelist (2 Timothy 4:5). It is, perhaps, a little surprising in his other lists of the spiritual gifts, Paul does not mention the gift of evangelism (see Romans 12:6 – 8 and 1 Corinthians 12:7 – 10 and 28 – 30).

This does not mean that Paul thought evangelism was not important. Paul probably does not mention the gift of evangelism in his lists about

---

11 Speaking of the Gospel writers as "Evangelists" is a common practice in Christian writings from the Second Century onwards. Papias of Hierapolis (c. 60 A.D. – 130 A.D.) called the apostle John whom he knew, "John the evangelist." Tertullian (c. 155 A.D. – c. 220 A.D.) in his "Answer to the Jews", uses the title "evangelist" when he quotes from Luke 16:6. He says, "And justly does the evangelist write, "The law and the prophets (were) until John the Baptist." In Chapter 36 of his "Prescription Against Heretics", speaking of the church Tertullian says, "the law and the prophets she unites in one volume with the writings of evangelists and apostles". In Chapter 23 of his work, "Against Praxeas" he speaks of, "the evangelist and beloved disciple John." Hippolytus of Rome (c. 170 A.D. – c. 235) in his commentary on Proverbs and also in his "Discourse On The Holy Theophany" refers to the Gospel writers as evangelists.

spiritual gifts because he just cannot imagine a Christian who does not do the work of an evangelist. Evangelism is at the core of Christian nature. Paul just expects all Christians will be evangelists. If this is the case, it gives weight to the idea that when Paul mentions evangelists in his list in Ephesians 4:11, he is referring to the four Gospel writers. If evangelism is fundamental to being Christian, it is hardly necessary to single it out as a specific gift unless Paul is referring to another gift. In this case, the gift of Christ to His church of the four Gospel writers. When Paul lists evangelists alongside apostles and prophets, he is most likely referring to the evangelists known as Matthew, Mark and Luke. It is not out of place for us to add the evangelist John once his Gospel is written.

PASTOR TEACHERS

Finally, I also need to say a word about *pastors and teachers*. I hope by now, by the way I have been referring to pastors and teachers, that you have discerned this phrase describes the one ministry in the gift of Christ. In this list of the ministries that make up the one gift of Christ, the phrase, *pastors and teachers* describes the one ministry. There is not one ministry of pastors and a different one of teachers. They are one and the same ministry. This seems to be the sense of Paul's meaning in the way he has phrased this list. The ESV gives a good sense of this translation. The two words (in the ESV, "shepherds and teachers") describe the nature of this ministry. The pastor, or shepherd, is a person who teaches. The teacher is a person who pastors or shepherds God's flock. This phrasing is very clear in the Greek text.[12]

This means that a pastor is a person who teaches.[13] The teaching a pastor does will be pastoral in its focus. The pastor will so teach that God's people are cared for and equipped for living. This is why pastoral care is the essence of pastoral ministry. Pastoral care is not something to add on to ministry so that we make sure people who find themselves in a crisis situation might have some special care. Pastoral care is about equipping the saints for the work of ministry, that is, for building the body of Christ. It is therefore a whole-of-life ministry.

This also means that the teacher is a person who pastorally cares for the flock. A teacher in the Christian church is not a person who delivers a dry, esoteric treatise. The teacher is a person who brings the word of God to bear on the people of God. This teaching will equip God's people to know God. It will equip God's people to build the body of Christ. It will equip the Christian person to live and work as a Christian person in the secular world. It will ensure that God's people have a respected voice in the public square. This is pastoral care. As Eugene Peterson has said, "I was not primarily dealing with people as problems. I was … calling them to worship God."[14]

---

12 In the Greek text the construction is μὲν … δὲ. Καὶ αὐτὸς ἔδωκεν τοὺς μὲν ἀποστόλους, τοὺς δὲ προφήτας, τοὺς δὲ εὐαγγελιστάς, τοὺς δὲ ποιμένας καὶ διδασκάλους, Notice τοὺς μὲν ἀποστόλους followed by τοὺς δὲ προφήτας and then τοὺς δὲ εὐαγγελιστάς and finally τοὺς δὲ ποιμένας καὶ διδασκάλους where the article and the final δὲ cover both ποιμένας καὶ διδασκάλους. I am not convinced by Arnold's argument on this verse in his Zondervan commentary on Ephesians. Clinton E. Arnold. *Ephesians (Zondervan Exegetical Commentary on The New Testament series Book 10)*. Zondervan Academic. Grand Rapids. 2010.
13 See 1 Timothy 3:1 – 13 for the qualifications of an overseer and deacon.
14 Winn Collier. *A Burning in My Bones – The Authorized Biography of Eugene H. Peterson*. (London. Authentic. 2022). 132.

Because pastor/teacher is one ministry in this list of the gift of Christ, the list (or the gift) contains four distinct ministries. They work together to equip the saints (the people of God) for the work of ministry which is to build the body of Christ. Just as the ministry of the pastor teacher is one, so the ministries of apostles, prophets and evangelists is one in that these three form the one sacred text of Scripture. The pastor teacher works closely with the apostles, prophets and evangelists. In other words, the pastor teacher works closely with the Scriptures and their proclamation. In practise this working closely will involve the pastor teacher helping the church of God deepen their understanding of the apostles', prophets' and evangelists' teaching. That is, the work of the pastor is to deepen the saints' understanding of the Scriptures and of its message proclaimed. This is pastoral care.

A Reformed theological position holds that preaching is proclaiming, on the one hand, and listening to, on the other, the word of God. I think, however, this position goes too far. Christian theology of every Christian denomination through the centuries has held that the word of God is that which is written in the Old and New Testaments. My heart has dropped on some occasions as I have opened my Bible to follow what the preacher was about to say. But these sermons have not explained the Scriptures. They have been speeches that made no coherent sense. I have wondered what the preacher thought they were doing. In the middle of one of these, the preacher answered his phone and had a discussion with his wife about what time he would be home. On other occasions I have heard preachers speak heresy. Such "preaching" is not the word of God.

We should hold a very high view of the sermon, but it is not the word of God. The sermon is an opportunity for the pastor teacher to help the saints have a deeper understanding of the Scriptures. Preaching is a solemn task and must not be taken lightly. A sermon must be prepared well, drawing on the preacher's theological training. The preacher must rightly handle the word of truth (2 Timothy 2:15). The sermon is not an opportunity just to give people a more thorough knowledge of the Scriptures. The sermon must focus on the pastoral care of people, equipping them for ministry in the church and in the world. The sermon must help God's people to live in this world with a focus on God's kingdom. This is pastoral care.

The preacher's task in preparing a sermon is to very carefully and properly understand the Scripture passage or topic in front of them. When I was 18 years old, I joined the Jay Cees, a community service organisation for young people between the ages of 18 and 40. A major thrust of the Jay Cees is to learn public speaking. By the time I was in my early 20s I could confidently get up in front of any crowd of any size and speak on almost any subject. When I started preaching, I lost that bold, youthful confidence because I realised that in a sermon I was trying to help people know God. In a sermon I am trying to rightly explain what the Bible says. This is serious business. I had to carefully understand the Bible passage in front of me and carefully prepare an explanation of it that would help people to know God. My fear was that if I got the message wrong, I would be sending people off to Hell rather than helping them to know God.

In preparing a sermon the preacher works hard to understand the text or topic. At the same time the preacher is constantly thinking about how this will help the congregation to know God more deeply. What does the passage have to say to the exhausted Christian mother to encourage her in her vital ministry? What does the passage say to the couple in relationship difficulties to help them to be subject to one another out of reverence for Christ (Ephesians 5:21)? What does the passage say to the Christian worker about how to be a *Christian* worker in the coming week? These are the sorts of questions pastor teachers apply themselves to in sermon preparation so that when they stand in the pulpit they will be exercising pastoral care of God's flock and be equipping the saints for the work of ministry, the building of the body of Christ.

BUILDING THE BODY

The focus of the work of ministry in Ephesians 4:12 is building the body of Christ. This word *building* (οἰκοδομὴ - oikodome) has the sense of *building, strengthening, encouraging*. When the apostle Paul uses this metaphor of the body of Christ, he is referring to the gathered community of believers. This is the local congregation, the local church. The members of the local church work together, much as a body does, for the wellbeing of all its members. Each member exercises their unique gifts for the benefit of all (see 1 Corinthians 12).

It is the *saints*, as Paul calls Christian people in Ephesians, who do this work of building, strengthening and encouraging. It is the word of God (apostles, prophets and evangelists) and pastor teachers who equip the saints for this ministry. The ministry pastor teachers do to equip the saints is the cure of souls or, pastoral care. You can see why pastoral care is a whole-of-life equipping activity.

To use Paul's image of the body from 1 Corinthians 12, pastoral care is about teaching the ear to be an ear, teaching an eye to be an eye etc. In other words, the role of pastoral care is to teach members of the congregation how to exercise their gift for the benefit of the whole body so that the church functions well. In Ephesians 4:13 the aim of the body working well together is to attain to the unity of the faith and of the knowledge of the Son of God. The whole thrust of what Paul is saying in Ephesians 4 is that we all grow together to be one as God is one.

In Ephesians 4:1 – 3 Paul has called on us to walk in a manner worthy of the calling to which we have been called, with all humility and gentleness, with patience, bearing with one another in love, eager to maintain the unity of the Spirit. This unity of the Spirit is something to maintain. We maintain this unity when we build, encourage and strengthen each other. Growing in this unity is growing in maturity. Growing in this unity expresses the nature of God to the world. As God is One in diversity, so God's people are one in diversity. This unity of Christians from all strata of society demonstrates to the world what God is like. Our unity in diversity demonstrates the love of God to a broken and divided world.

In Ephesians 4:4 – 5 Paul encourages us to maintain our unity by appealing to the trinitarian nature of God. He says, "There is one body and one Spirit—just as you were called to the one hope that belongs to your call— one Lord, one faith, one baptism, one God and Father of all, who is over all and through all and in all." (ESV). Just as God is one Spirit, one Lord and one God and Father so, we are one body. Being one with our brothers and sisters in the church is not just a nice idea. It's not someone's concoction to get us to get along with each other. Being one reflects the nature of God. Being unified as God's people will mean that when the unbeliever comes amongst us, they will say that God is truly with us (cf. 1 Corinthians 14:24 – 25).

The role of the pastor teacher is to help God's people to show this unity we have in Christ as the saints build the body. The church of God is made up of a diverse lot of people. And when I say, "the Church of God", I mean the local congregation. Coming together in unity expresses the nature of God. As a whole-of-life ministry, the ministry of the pastor teacher will be pastorally caring for the flock of God by encouraging us to reflect the nature and unity of God in our gatherings. From all our diverse backgrounds we will be one in Christ. Our unity will speak to the world about the nature of God.

CONCLUSION

The issues discussed in this chapter have been included to give a sense of what pastoral ministry is and how the essence of the role of the pastor teacher is pastoral care. Everything the pastor is involved in must have as its focus the *cure of souls*. At the same time this *cure of souls* must be based clearly on the Scriptures. God has given us the Scriptures, and pastors to equip us for ministry and to build the body of Christ.[15] Having a good theological education means that the pastor teacher will be seen as the expert in theology. This is not about being superior. It is not about being the academic in the pulpit. It means that in their ministry, pastor

---

15   If we look at Ephesians 4:11 in the following layout:
    v. 1. He gave
        v. 2a apostles, prophets, evangelists,
        v .2b pastors and teachers,
    v. 3a to equip the saints
        v. 3b with a view to work of ministry
        v. 3c with a view to building the body of Christ
we see that the reason Christ has given apostles etc., is to equip the saints. The reason Christ wants the saints equipped is twofold. Firstly, Christ wants them to do the work of ministry. Secondly, he wants them to build the body. For this layout, I am grateful to the Rev Dr Raymond Heslehurst in private correspondence.

teachers will be communicating to God's people that their pastoral care is based on a careful understanding of the Scriptures. The pastor teacher is a theologian.

The next chapter explains the role of the pastor teacher as a pastor theologian, so that when we think of pastors as teachers, we understand that what they will teach us is theology, not psychology or self-help or any other lesser thing. Thomas Aquinas said that theology is the, "Queen of the Sciences". What better description is there than that this one thing that will teach us the most important thing in life is called "theology", meaning, "words about God"? When we speak of the pastor teacher, we mean that the pastor will teach theology. The pastor will speak words to us about God. Anything less will fail to equip the saints for ministry. Anything less will not build the body of Christ. Anything less will not be pastoral care.

I was present for a minister's valedictory service in a church he had served for the past several years. I asked him what Bible passage he was going to preach on, expecting that, like the apostle Paul in his farewell to the elders of the church in Ephesus (Acts 20:17 – 38) he might want to give words of encouragement to stay faithful to the gospel message and to be on the lookout for false teachers who would inevitably come, seeking to destroy the flock of Christ. He said that he was just going to tell them stories. And so, he recalled incidents and stories over the past years, none of which encouraged the saints to reflect theologically on their lives and how they might approach the future, under God, to remain faithful. Not once did he refer God's people to God's word. It was a sad occasion because a vital opportunity was missed. This minister had not done the work of a pastor. He had failed to teach God's people to think theologically. He had not been pastorally caring for the flock of Christ.

The core of Christian ministry then, is pastoral care. This care is given to us by Christ's gift of apostles, prophets, and evangelists in the written word of God, and by pastor teachers, who lovingly teach us the word of God. Pastoral care is the pastor being a theologian, knowing the word of God and teaching the saints the word of God. There is no other way to equip the saints for ministry. There is no other way to build the body of Christ.

2

THE PASTOR THEOLOGIAN – GETTING THE BALANCE RIGHT AND WHY WE DON'T

THEOLOGY IN PASTORAL CARE

If you're going to give people pastoral care, you need to be a theologian. Yes, I really do mean that. In chapter one I have spoken about the sermon and the importance of understanding the Bible and of applying it in a real way to people's real situations. The pastor teacher should think of their sermon as an exercise in pastoral care. It is not an opportunity to show your erudite learning. It is an opportunity to draw alongside the people of God, to be with them in life and to equip them for the work of building the body of Christ. You can't do this if you are not trained in theology. To be trained in theology you do not necessarily need a degree from a seminary. I know some people who have been so well taught in their church that they have a deeper theological understanding than some preachers I've heard. But my point remains. Pastoral care needs theology.

Unfortunately, I have seen several pastors who have received excellent theological education yet do not seem to have a pastoral bone in their body. It is these disturbing scenes in part which have prompted me to write this book. I don't think you can be a pastor without being a theologian. I don't think you can be a theologian without being a pastor. If you have been taught the wonderful things of God, how can your soul not be stirred to want to share these things with others? Having delved deeply into the Scriptures' teaching on the grace of God towards a sinful people, how can you not want others to know there is hope in the world? How can your great theological understanding not stir you to bring comfort and encouragement to a hurting world? How can your theology and your pastoral care be divorced from one another?

To be a pastor teacher we need to have a very careful balance between pastoring and teaching. A pastor teacher who has their theology correct but can't translate it so the saints are equipped for building the body of Christ is not doing their job as a pastor teacher. The pastor teacher who has a deep compassion for people but doesn't know how to bring the comfort and encouragement of the Scriptures to real, everyday life situations, is not doing the job of a pastor teacher. Our theology and our pastoral care need to be fully integrated for us to perform the role of pastor teacher. Pastor teachers need to be pastor theologians.

At the end of four years in seminary a young man took up the role of assistant minister in a local church. His senior minister advised him to, "Forget all that stuff you learned in college. It doesn't work in the real world." Now, the senior minister was a good man. He loved to see people won to Christ. He had real care for people and wanted to bring Christ's compassion to bear on their lives. He worked hard to preach well and faithfully in his Sunday sermons. His belief that all the stuff we learned in college didn't work in the real world was, in fact, simply an expression that he had not worked out how to integrate his theology with his practice. His pastor's heart gave him the desire to bring the comfort and encouragement of the gospel to people in a hurting world, but he hadn't worked out how to translate the Bible into the messiness of life. That is not to say that his sermons were not faithfully teaching people the truths of the Bible. What he was not doing was the work of the pastor theologian, speaking God's truth into the lives of people so that they were better able to live as Christ's own in this messy world.

The balance I am suggesting to you between theological knowledge and loving care is not an easy thing to achieve. It takes work and awareness. In the novel *Gilead* by Marilynne Robinson there is a discussion between the unbelieving son of a pastor and another pastor about the doctrine of predestination. It's an awkward discussion and no solution is offered as to how a pastor who holds to this doctrine might communicate its truth meaningfully to an unbeliever. Integration of theology and pastoral care has not been done and because of it the words of the senior pastor who said, "the stuff you learn in college doesn't work in the real world," are true in this case. If you haven't integrated your theology and your pastoral practice the things you have learned in college won't work in the real world.

One great difficulty those who have a good theological education suffer from is that they are taught to be teachers. They see their role as a minister as teaching people God's truth. This is a very worthy thing to be wanting to do in ministry but, where it's not balanced with a real understanding of and skill in pastoral care it will struggle to equip the saints for building the body of Christ.

I remember the day a new couple turned up at church. This church was in a tourist destination, and we often had people on holiday come to church. This couple were on holiday and told me they would be moving on the next day. They told me they had stopped going to church in their hometown for various reasons and they thought that at this season of their life the Lord was OK with that. Now, let me say that theologically I have huge problems with such an attitude. If you're a Christian, you go to church. It's a no-brainer. I base my view on Hebrews 10:24 – 25. The writer of this letter says, "don't neglect to meet together." It's a no-brainer. John Stott puts it very bluntly in his book, *The Living Church – The convictions of a lifelong pastor* (IVP, 2007, 2021). He speaks of, "that grotesque anomaly, an unchurched Christian." (p. 19).

With Hebrews 10:24 – 25 ringing alarm bells in my head, I put on my pastoral care hat and tried to empathise and understand with this couple what was really going on for them. They responded well, I thought, to my caring, pastoral concern for them. I felt it was a difficult conversation as I tried to negotiate my theology and the situation of a couple of God's children who were clearly hurting about their home church situation.

As we talked on, and the couple seemed to appreciate my care for them, it became clear time was running short and they needed to move on. Realising this would probably be the last time I would see this couple, I became anxious that, despite my great skills in pastoral care, they had not yet come around to seeing the danger they were in by giving up meeting with God's people. So, because time had become short, I quickly whipped off my pastoral care hat and put on my teaching hat. I pointed them to the passage in Hebrews. At once their mood changed. They shut down. I had defaulted to being the teacher with the great theological education. I had not integrated my theology with my pastoral practice.

The problem for me was that I had forced a wedge into my role and divided pastoral care and teaching. Notice that I, "whipped off my pastoral care hat and put on my teaching hat." For the pastor teacher, there are not two hats. There is the one hat of pastoring and teaching.

At this point I can hear some of you saying to me that if I am not teaching the Word of God I am not pastorally caring for people. I agree with you. But look back over that encounter I had with this couple who had stopped going to church. Did what I say to them encourage them to start going to church again? No, it didn't. In fact, I failed in my responsibility to teach them the Word of God. Yes, I mouthed what the scriptures say, but did I *teach* them? These days, I lecture in a theological college, and I know that if my students haven't understood the lesson, I have not really taught them. If they haven't understood the words from my mouth, they have not learned the lesson that day. In order to be the teacher a pastor is, we need to integrate our theology with our pastoral practice. Folk will often not hear our wonderful teaching if we don't bring it to them in a pastorally sensitive way.

I was watching a YouTube channel which engages pastors in conversation. On this occasion the host made this wonderful statement, "We as pastors need to encourage beautifully, sensitively, with scripture to the heart and the Spirit will take it from there." I like the idea of "beautifully and sensitively" applying Scripture to the heart. Would that all pastoring and teaching did this. Sometimes we can think it is most important to teach God's truth that we lose all sense of pastorally caring for the saints, as I did with the visiting couple at church that morning. When we do this, it is easy to blame the Holy Spirit for our mistakes. The thought is that, as a pastor teacher, I have a responsibility to teach God's people God's truth. If they don't like my beautiful and sensitive words, I can't be held responsible, but if the Holy Spirit is doing His part, they will see the truth of what I am teaching. On the contrary, if they haven't understood my pastoral teaching, I can't blame the Holy Spirit for not doing His part. I need to take my responsibilities as a pastor teacher more seriously and look more carefully at how I integrate my teaching with my pastoral care. The Holy Spirit will still do His part, but I need to do mine as well.

It is the responsibility of the pastor teacher to beautifully and sensitively teach God's people God's truth but, in doing so our focus needs to be on the person we are teaching. It is no good to say at the end of a sermon or a pastoral conversation, "Well, I got that right." The questions we need to answer are these: "Did I teach God's truth in such a way that God's people were cared for? Were God's people so moved by my pastoral care that they came to a deeper understanding of the things of God? Did my teaching and caring equip the saints to build the body of Christ?" The thing I did wrong with the visiting couple was that I put my need to teach God's truth above caring for a couple in difficulties. I had not yet come to an understanding of the process which had led them to stop attending church. Pastor teachers need to understand our people for our pastoring and teaching to be effective. As soon as I switched from pastoring this couple to making sure they were told God's truth, I saw a visible change in their demeanour. They shut down. They were no longer able to hear anything I was saying.

Integrating theology and pastoral care is a difficult business. The work of the pastor theologian requires hard work. It begins with focusing on the person, assuming you have already done the hard work of being theologically trained. Pastoral care does not focus on the problem. It does not look at the problem of a couple not attending church and then try to fix the problem. Pastoral care looks at the couple and concentrates on the process. *Process* is about what is going on for the person. It has to do, not with the problem, but with how the person is handling their situation. Each of us will deal with life's situations differently. Someone will not cope well with a situation that another person will thrive in. How each of us cope with life's situations is how we *process* the situation. One person will welcome the challenge, another will crumble under the weight of it. *Process* is a topic all its own. I will leave it for a fuller discussion in Chapter Six.

WHY WE LOSE THE BALANCE – AND HOW TO AVOID IT

Some of the scenes I have witnessed of a pastor doing a terrible job of caring for a member of God's flock are because the pastor is worn out. This is often referred to as "burn out". They are suffering from compassion fatigue. Statistics indicate that about half our clergy leave ministry altogether. A substantial number of the ministers who leave do so because of burn out. To help clergy not burn out and leave a ministry they once believed God had led them into, clergy need to submit themselves to a process of pastoral supervision or spiritual direction. We need to have another godly person who can look at us and our ministry more objectively than we can ourselves, to advise us, encourage us, direct us and hold us so that our great desire to care for God's flock doesn't become something we run away from or that wears us down so that we become ineffective.

We need to be clear on what pastoral supervision is. It is not having someone supervise our work. Pastoral supervision is not about having an overseer direct what we do, telling us what we have done right or wrong. Pastoral supervision looks at the process. The Australasian

Association of Supervision (AAOS) says, "Supervision is an opportunity for the supervisee [the pastoral carer] to reflect on their practice to gain a broader perspective, opening up a space in which to discover possibilities for personal and professional growth." Supervision is distinct from coaching, mentoring and spiritual direction. AAOS defines supervision as a "contractual, relational, collaborative process, which facilitates the ethical and professional practice of the supervisee" and goes on to say, "The supervisor provides a space to ensure the supervisee is accountable to the personal and professional standards of their profession."[16] In practice, a supervisor facilitates a person in looking objectively at their ministry and exploring how this ministry is impacting the pastor personally, professionally and ethically. The supervisor will facilitate the pastor in developing better practice in ministry.

Pastoral supervision helped me to look more objectively at the process of my encounter with the couple on holiday. Sitting face to face with a pastoral supervisor and discussing the process of this encounter helped me see more objectively where my own fears (of failing to faithfully teach the word of God) stopped the pastoral process dead in its tracks.

Let's return to the conversation with the pastor I watched on the YouTube channel. The conversation was in the context of the aftermath of COVID-19 lockdowns. Our governments had directed that churches were not to meet. Most of us jumped into online church. But then, as restrictions were eased and people started meeting again, our numbers in attendance at church did not return to what they had been before the lockdowns. The pastor mentioned some people in his congregation who had not returned to physically meeting with the rest of their church.

---

16 See the AAOS web site: https://www.supervision.org.au/what-is-supervision/

He mentioned one particular elderly man and was asked by the host to roleplay how he might pastorally care for this man to encourage him to return to church. The pastor roleplayed the conversation like this:

Pastor: "Bob, haven't seen you for a while. How are you going?"

Man: "I haven't been coming to church because I haven't been out of the house. We've been doing on-line shopping and everything. I just don't feel comfortable."

Pastor: "So when will you re-engage with the world, with your brothers and sisters in Christ? What will have to change before you're happy to do that again? Because this could go on for a year or more."

Man: "I guess when the numbers go down further."

Pastor: "Australia has the best numbers. But really others in a high-risk category have started coming again. Don't let fear prevent you when we're working really hard to address the risks."

I hope when you read this roleplay, very loud alarm bells are ringing in your head and in your pastor's heart. Please keep in mind that the pastor was asked, without any warning to perform a roleplay, with no preparation, while the cameras were rolling. So, I am being a bit unkind to pick on it. I'm not sure I would have done better under the circumstances, but the roleplay illustrates the point. What we read in this roleplay are the words of a teacher. They are not the words of a pastor. The pastor in this roleplay has not heard what the man has said to him. He has not responded to the real concern the man has expressed. The pastor has engaged in this conversation it seems, with the sole purpose of getting the man back to church. That is not pastoral care. Yes, the man needs to get back to church for his own wellbeing and the benefit of his fellow believers as they consider how to stir up one another to love and good works. But the pastor in this roleplay has completely ignored the fears the man has expressed. The pastor's response is to basically tell the man he is being unrealistic. "When will you re-engage? This [pandemic] could go on for years." The pastor's response also tells the man he is being ignorant. "Australia has the best numbers." This response seems to be saying that if the man knew the real situation, he wouldn't be afraid. The pastor has shown no pastoral care in this.

The response in this roleplay would have begun to show some pastoral care if the pastor had acknowledged the man's fears. Whether the pastor thinks these fears are realistic or not, they are real for the man. Pastoral care will acknowledge the man's reality. It is so empowering, if we are feeling a particular emotion, when someone comes alongside us, acknowledges our emotion, and gives us the sense that it's OK to be feeling that emotion. Our emotion may not be rational, and we might even be aware that it's not rational, but for someone to sit with us, to not fear our emotion, we feel not alone, and the emotion loses some of its power. The pastor doesn't need to understand the emotion. He might even think it's a silly emotional response to a particular situation, but it is the reality the person is feeling, and *that* is what the pastor must understand and communicate that it's OK.

Because you have been a good pastor theologian and taught your congregation well, this man in the roleplay already knows he should not stop meeting together, as some are in the habit of doing. You don't need to teach him that again. Once you have acknowledged his real fear and communicated to him that it's OK to feel that way, he feels safe. In this place of safety, you could then raise the issue of physical church attendance by asking how, in the light of Hebrews 10:24 – 25, the man could sit more lightly with his fear. Having said that, it is only through *process* that you will be pastorally able to encourage the man to come to a position where he is able to address his behaviour. So, please pay particular attention to Chapter Six about process.

I have mentioned the reason a lot of pastoral care fails is because the pastor is burnt out or suffering from compassion fatigue. Once, while I was visiting a church, I observed a conversation between the senior minister and a member of the congregation. We were standing around at morning tea after the morning service. The minister approached a man in his 40s and asked how he was. This man did not take this to be a polite greeting and told his minister he was devastated. He said he had just discovered that his 18-year-old son had developed a drug habit and had been stealing money from the family to pay for it. The minister's response was, "I'm sorry to hear that. If there's anything I can do, let me know." He then walked away.

TOO MUCH BUSINESS

This minister was so burdened by the business of doing church that in his response to a heartfelt need of a member of God's flock he did more harm than good. One mistake the minister made was to ask about what he could do. Pastoral care is not about *doing*. It is about *being*. The business of running a church takes us away from being a pastor teacher. Churches need running and in most that burden often falls to the senior minister. There are meetings to arrange, buildings to repair and trades people to organise, disputes in the choir to resolve, visits to be made, reports to be sent, finances to be worried about. Most of these do not involve the cure of souls. But they are easy to retreat into, to convince yourself and the congregation that you are busy looking after the church.

The ministry of the pastor teacher is not to run a church. The ministry of the pastor teacher is to be with the saints. That is the essence of pastoring. Being with people. This *being* is about bringing the teaching of the scriptures to bear in ordinary people's lives, in the ordinary places they live and work. Senior ministers are often burdened by the business of church and can find they become anxious about the large amount of administrative work they need to do. This work must not become the priority for the pastor teacher. The pastor teacher needs to be able to move from what they thought would be a pleasant chat over morning tea to drawing alongside a hurting father and to share something of that burden. They need to be able to do this with no feeling of guilt that there are so many things to do. It's not about doing. It's about being. In one sense, hearing at morning tea that one of the saints is hurting badly and wants you to draw alongside, should bring with it a great sense of relief. You now won't have time to do those reports for the denominational hierarchy. The Bishop can wait! You have an urgent need to be with a member of God's church. Administration will just have to take a back seat. There is a vital need to draw alongside and be the pastor teacher.

When a friend of mine started as pastor at a new church there were no other staff at all. There was no other minister, no administrative help, no one to tend the grounds or do maintenance or cleaning. In this situation most clergy would think the first staff appointment to make would be an assistant minister. Someone who can share the burden of pastoral care, so the senior minister is not overwhelmed. Instead, my friend's first staff appointment was an administrative assistant. This freed him from some of the burden of running the church, which, because of his pastoral focus, he believed was not where he should exert his energies. Appointing an administrative assistant gave him more time to exercise pastoral care, the very thing he was appointed to the church to do.

Most clergy would feel some fear and inadequacy if confronted by a situation at morning tea where a parishioner tells us they are in crisis. Most of us would think about what to do next. But remember, there is nothing to do. We just have to be. Be alongside one of the saints whose world has just turned upside down. That doesn't mean we say nothing. And it certainly doesn't mean we walk away. It means we express real empathy. We recognise one of God's flock is hurting in a way we may not understand or in a way we have never experienced. Or, maybe we have experienced a similar situation. In this case we need to be especially careful that the focus does not turn to us. When we draw alongside a person our focus must remain with the person. We cannot be distracted onto what might once have happened to ourselves. We cannot be distracted by other things going on around us or the church business that so urgently needs our attention.

Do you believe in the sovereignty of God? If God has placed this hurting person before you, that's where you're meant to be. That's the place God wants you to be. You are not meant to be doing church business. You are meant to be taking up the cure of souls.

BEING WITH PEOPLE

How do you be with a person who is hurting? You show them firstly you are not scared of their situation. You are not horrified or judgemental about any immorality or other sinful behaviour. This does not mean you communicate that sinful acts do not matter. It means you acknowledge that something wrong has happened but, for the moment, we just sit with it, we grieve in its presence together. The fact that you have absolutely no idea of what to do next to solve their issue is not important. The fact of just being in their reality is empowering.

To pastorally care for a person our focus stays with the person. Imagine if we said to the man at morning tea, "Oh, I understand. When my son was 18, he did the same thing." This is not empathy. Our focus has shifted from the person in crisis. We are no longer alongside in their crisis. We have moved into our own world. It is really the same thing as saying, "Tell me if there's anything I can do," and then walking away. Starting to talk about my experience is saying to the other person, "I'm not really interested in what's happening to you. Here's what happened to me." It has the same effect as walking away. It communicates, "I am not interested."

On two separate occasions when two friends of mine faced crisis situations very similar to situations I had been in myself, I said to my friends, "I understand". Both of them responded with, "No, you don't." It took these two rebukes, separated by a couple of years, for me to get the point. In pastoral care, it's not about me. Keep your focus on the other.

In keeping our focus on the other our own experience matters very little. At best, if we have had similar experiences to what the other person is going through, it will help us to know that people come out the other end. Our experience will help us to know there is hope. We will be able to sit with the other person without feeling out of control. We will not feel threatened by their crisis because, having been through something similar, we know there is hope.

Avoid saying, "I understand." Whatever situation we have been through, it will have differences to that which the person we're now talking with is going through. Their situation is different. They will also react differently to their situation than we did to ours. Our task is to listen to their story and not introduce our story.

Saying, "I understand," also brings the focus back onto me and my experience. We want to keep focused on the other person so that they feel we are with them and that we are listening to and understanding their story and the way they have reacted to the events they have experienced. This is empathy.

Some years ago, I spoke with a pastor who had met a husband and wife from my congregation while they were all on holidays. Over the course of their conversations the pastor told this couple how he and his wife were trying to cope within themselves over the recent loss of their two-year-old daughter. The pastor told me how they listened to him without giving advice, without trying to tell him things would be OK, without saying insensitive things like, "Well, at least she's with the Lord now." The pastor told me how helpful those conversations had been, just because the couple listened. They were not frightened by the topic but engaged with real empathy. I said to the pastor that I was pleased this couple had been helpful and I told him they had, themselves, lost a two-year-old some years previously. The pastor responded with understanding, "That's why they were so helpful to me."

The point to note in this conversation between the pastor and the husband and wife is that the couple never told the pastor about their experience. At that point, their experience was not important for the pastor to hear while dealing with his own grief. But their experience was important for it gave them empathy and the confidence to pastorally care for the pastor in his grief.

Sometimes you may find the other person asks you about your experience.

They may know you have experienced something similar and ask you how you coped with it. In this case feel free to share your experience. You have been asked for it. But do so in a manner that keeps the focus on the other. You don't want the pastoral conversation becoming all about you. Your aim in a pastoral conversation is always to help someone see how God is in their situation with them. This aim of pastoral care is discussed more fully in Chapter Four.

Sometimes, as I have sat with people, listening to their struggles, they have looked up and said, "But there are people worse off than me." This may be an attempt to say, "I don't want to talk anymore. I'm sick of feeling this pain." I have found that it is more often than not because the person hasn't yet confronted the real source of their pain. I have, therefore, responded with something like, "That's probably true (that there are people in harder situations) but that doesn't mean you haven't got real pain." Saying something like this has helped people to acknowledge that with all the issues going on around them, the real issue to deal with is the personal pain they are feeling. Their focus needs to move from the events happening to them to the process happening within them. When a person suggests others are worse off, of course, that may be very true, but they still have to deal with their own situation. Pastoral care will help them to look at the process they are going through.

For the theologically trained pastor, getting the balance right, between being the pastor and the theologian, will help the saints grow to maturity. Your good theology will teach them about God and what He has done for us in Christ. Your well-practiced pastoral care will help them negotiate the vicissitudes of life to discover how God is with them and how to be Christian in the world.

PASTOR THEOLOGIAN – EQUIPPING THE SAINTS FOR LIFE

Being Christian in the world is part of what Christians are asking their pastors to do when they ask them to get Sunday right. We'll discuss "getting Sunday right" more fully in Chapter Five, but the average Christian, who interacts with ordinary people in all aspects of life during the week, wants to know how to live as a Christian in the secular world. They want to have a positive Christian influence in the life of their families, friends, neighbours and colleagues. They are asking their pastors to equip them for this ministry when they ask them to get Sunday right. Christian people also want to be equipped to have a positive Christian response to the issues people in the public square are grappling with. They want to be able to engage intelligently in debates about life's issues. They want to be a Christian voice among the many competing voices of the 21st century.

Equipping God's people to have a Christian voice in the public square is the role of the pastor teacher as a pastor theologian. In the book, *Becoming a Pastor Theologian: New Possibilities for Church Leadership*, Peter J. Leithart in his chapter entitled, "The Pastor Theologian as Biblical Theologian – From the Church for the Church", says, "Ecclesial biblical theologians are … inevitably, naturally, public and political theologians."[17] Leithart's contention is that theology has become an academic exercise. Theology is often the academy speaking to the academy. Rather, theology needs to be the pastor teacher equipping the saints for the work of ministry. Pastor theologians equip the saints to interact, naturally in the public and political world. This also means that when teaching theology, our seminaries need to speak to pastoral care. The academy needs

---

17 Todd Wilson and Gerald Hiestand (Eds.) *Becoming a Pastor Theologian: New Possibilities for Church Leadership* (p. 20). InterVarsity Press. 2016. Kindle Edition.

to speak to the world where pastoral care takes place.

When people think of theology, their minds instinctively turn to the academic world of the seminary, theological college or Bible college. Leithart argues that pastors have a responsibility to bring theology to the pews. They must equip the saints to think theologically about the world. My contention is that this task is an essential task of the pastor teacher. The pastor teacher is a pastor theologian who thinks theologically about the world which members of their congregation inhabit every day. The pastor theologian will teach the saints also to think theologically about their daily existence so they can bring a Christian voice into that world.

This Christian thinking, this theological or biblical thinking, is not providing proof texts for people to quote in various situations. It is not about providing trite answers to difficult questions. It is about having a deep knowledge of Scripture, understanding the sweep of biblical revelation. This biblical knowledge equips the saints to develop a Christian mind, to think Christianly about the world they inhabit and to have a Christian voice in it.

Memorising verses and passages of Scripture is a good thing to do but having a deeper knowledge of the full sweep of Scripture helps us to think Christianly about life. Caring for the souls of God's people, the pastor teacher will teach this full sweep. They will teach God's people to think Christianly about their lives. This ministry takes time and hard work. If you're looking for a relaxed and contemplative life in ministry, it's probably best that you look for something else to do. If you believe God wants you as part of His gift to equip the saints for the work of ministry, be prepared to work hard. The ministry of a pastor teacher is not only demanding of time but also requires rigorous work in the study and with the people. The pastor teacher is well trained in theology and has worked out how to translate that theology to equip the saints to have a respected Christian voice in the secular world. This is the balance needed in pastoral care.

This work of the pastor teacher with the people takes time. It involves spending time with the people you pastor. While it may involve having a pleasant cup of tea with a godly older Christian, from whom we will usually learn more about a godly life than we will teach, it is never only about a cup of tea. As a pastor teacher, your role is to equip. Over a pleasant cup of tea, you will be listening. You will be pastorally listening to this saint, not just so that you will be blessed, though there is nothing wrong with you being blessed by a member of God's congregation. These times of blessing relieve some of the stress that comes our way in ministry. But as a pastor teacher, you will be listening for ways you can equip this saint for the work of building the body of Christ. You will be listening for ways you can bring the comfort and encouragement of the Lord to them. It may be that their work of building the body of Christ is in the blessing they bring to their pastor. There is nothing wrong with encouraging this older saint to continue this ministry. It benefits you and therefore the congregation at the same time. But keep on listening. This older saint may have other needs.

As a pastor spending time with God's people, you will do so in a large variety of situations. It will not all be a pleasant cup of tea with a retired person in their 80s. You will be grabbing a quick bite of lunch with the busy executive downtown, you will spend time with the young couple and their family in their hectic chaos. You will help the farmer milk their cows. You will spend time surfing with members of the congregation. In one day you will have lunch with the chairman of the Stock Exchange and spend the evening in a smoke filled room of young people discussing life, the universe and everything. You interact with your people in the ordinariness of their lives. You spend time with God's people whatever activities form part of their lives. As their pastor, you will be listening, getting to know their lives. Getting to know the issues they confront each day. And as you listen you will be thinking, doing the hard work of the pastor theologian to help bring a biblical perspective into these lives. You will be translating the Bible into their language, the language of the ordinariness of their lives.

Pastor teachers will not only be spending time with God's people in their activities and in the world they inhabit so that you get to know them. You will also be spending time listening to the issues of the world in which God's people live. God's people want to be able to respond Christianly to worldly issues and events. It is the pastor teacher's responsibility to equip God's people to be able to make these Christian responses.

What has been happening in the Western world for some time now is that the world is rapidly moving away from living by a Christian ethic within a Christian world view. In many places abortion has become an accepted practice for birth control. Most Western nations have changed the definition of marriage so that a couple are no longer bound together in holy matrimony. The right of the individual to demand that others acknowledge their personal beliefs about their identity has triumphed over the concept of identity as a person in God's image. What does the Christian voice say to this world today?

It is the responsibility of the pastor teacher to equip God's congregation to have a Christian voice in the world. Pastor teachers have the responsibility to speak with a Christian voice in a way the world will understand.

In practice, there seems to be two different reactions Christians have to these developments in the West. One reaction is to just state loudly what we think is a Christian understanding. This type of response usually is not effective because it ends up being two different world views yelling at each other across a great divide, over which no one can pass.

Another reaction arises out of, what seems to me to be, a false understanding of Christian compassion. In our desire to accept every person as God has accepted us, many Christians have given up a Christian ethic and world view and have taken on the values of the world. This is one of the saddest results of pastor teachers losing sight of their role as pastor theologians. It is our responsibility to spend time teaching God's people how to have an informed response to the world, how to bring a Christian ethic and world view into the public square. This is pastoral care.

It is the responsibility of the pastor theologian to equip the saints so that they have a recognised, welcomed and reasoned voice in the public square. We live in a political world and Christians need to, and want to, participate in our political debates. It is the responsibility of their pastor to equip them with a Christian voice that recognises there is a clash of world views when Christians speak into a secular world. Our Christian voice needs to understand how to build bridges between the competing ideas of these worlds so that we are at least communicating, and we have some understanding of each other's world view. It is a travesty when Christians do not have a thought-out position and end up taking on the values the world promotes. This has happened in some places with the same sex marriage debate as well as male female relationships.

Taking the second of these as an illustration, I have recently been involved in debates about the relationships between men and woman and the role of male headship. This is not the place to pursue this issue in any depth, but there is research which shows that domestic violence is higher in homes where the family attends a church that teaches male headship. Many members of my Denomination have therefore said we must stop teaching male headship. This response is the travesty I see of Christians giving in to a secular voice because we have not thought through the issue with a Christian mind. My strong opposition to being told I must stop teaching male headship is because the Bible teaches male headship (see 1 Corinthians 11:3 and Ephesians 5:23 in their contexts). The task of the pastor theologian is not to stop teaching what the Bible says because the world says there is a problem with it. If it is true that the rate of domestic violence is higher in homes where the family attends a church that teaches male headship (and I have no reason to doubt the statistics), the solution is not to give up teaching what the Bible says. The solution is to make sure we understand what the Bible truly says and to faithfully teach it. We must also confront domestic violence with biblical teaching about the role of husbands and wives (Husbands, love your wives as Christ loves the church and gave himself for her, Ephesians 5:25. He doesn't hit us, psychologically abuse us or gaslight us.)

These issues are laden with emotion. It is not an easy task to address them but addressing them is the task of the pastor theologian. God's people want to know how to make a godly response to the issues the world faces. The pastor theologian will faithfully teach them how to live in the world and to have a godly response to its issues. This is pastoral care.

The issue of family violence being more prevalent in Christian homes that teach male headship is a travesty. A Christian home should be a place of safety, nurture and love. That a Christian home might be a place of violence is contempt of Christ. Domestic violence in a Christian home is a mockery of Christ's relationship with His people. How can any husband who understands his role is to love his wife as Christ loves the church, be violent towards his wife? How is this disconnect possible? Where are our pastor theologians carefully teaching the balance of headship and service?

The pastor theologian will tackle some controversial issues. Your desire will be to give God's congregation a biblical world view on the issues society is grappling with and to encourage them to obey scriptural teaching in their own lives. The pastor doesn't take sides in public debate. Inevitably it will be clear biblical teaching has more affinity with one side than another. What must be clear is that any bias arises out of the Scriptures and not from the pastor's own political preferences.

Predictably pastors will find there are members of the congregation who disagree with them. This is a good thing. It means the pastor is not on a pedestal. While the congregation should rightly acknowledge the pastor is an expert in theology this does not mean the pastor is the authority to obey. The *Priesthood of all Believers* teaches that all Christians have access to the Bible. It is not the exclusive domain of a particular caste of God's people. A pastor who is comfortable in their role will welcome robust debate with members of the congregation. Ultimately each Christian must follow their own, biblically informed, conscience before God. Pastoral care is teaching God's people the whole counsel of God. It is not lauding it over people.

AVOIDING PHARISAIC OBEDIENCE

Pastor teachers as pastor theologians teach God's people to rightly live out a balanced Christian life. One verse or one passage of Scripture is not promoted above another to force a wrong understanding of Christian living. But the pastor theologian must be careful that God's people do not fall into the same self-righteousness that the Pharisees of Jesus' time did. They kept the minutiae of the Law but ignored the fact that the Law was made for the benefit of humanity, not humanity for the Law (see Mark 2:27).

Pastor theologians can teach all they like about good Christian behaviour and give the impression "we are not like that" (those who express violence, for example). But we need to be realistic. There will be homes represented in God's congregation where violence and anger and other sinful behaviour exists. Congregations need to establish an attitude of caring and helpfulness for those in trouble, not one of condemnation, judgement and exclusion. Remember, we are under grace and we treat people with grace. This is where the pastor teacher exercises real pastoral care. We have clear guidance from God how to live in His world. We can teach very carefully the nuances of Scripture so members of God's church don't hold one part over against another. But we need to be careful we don't train people up to be pharisaic law keepers. Life is messy. We must learn to live with the mess in a godly and gracious way always seeking to clean up the mess.

Some years ago, I visited a church that had a roll book with photographs of all its members. As I was looking through this book the pastor said to me, "You will notice we have a number of divorced people in our church. That's because we don't shoot our wounded." A pastor teacher will never condone sin in God's people but at the same time they will not shoot the wounded. Pastor teachers live with the messiness of life while at the same time work hard as pastor theologians to equip the saints for ministry with a right understanding and application of Scripture.

Pastor theologians teach the Bible. Leave the self-help and prosperity stuff to those who get paid the big bucks. To equip the saints, we need to teach the Bible. I don't mean the sermon should be a Bible study. In the sermon you don't need to show how hard you have worked on the Greek or Hebrew text in preparation. The sermon is not the place to discuss Greek grammar. Preaching and equipping the saints is to teach the whole sweep of Biblical theology in such a way that God's people will know how the whole of biblical revelation applies to their everyday living.[18]

Leithart argues that the greatest risk to the church is not opposition from the world but from liberal theology. The risk to godly behaviour that strives to follow the Scriptures does not come from the world but from those within who have already capitulated to the ungodly immorality of the world and encourage others to do the same. We should not be surprised that this is the case. Both the apostles Peter and Paul warned us about it (2 Peter 2:1 – 3 and Acts 20:29).

The false teachers of today argue that, for the sake of the mission of the church, Christians must change with the world and be relevant to people who live in a 21st century scientific culture. They argue that modern secular psychology has given us insights into the human condition that were not available to the biblical writers. We must therefore leave behind these primitive understandings, they say, and get with the agenda of the modern world. These false teachers have lost confidence in the word of

---

18 For a detailed discussion of the role of Pastor Theologians as ecclesial, biblical theologians who are public and political theologians see Peter J. Leithart, "The Pastor Theologian as Biblical Theologian - From the Church for the Church" in Todd Wilson & Gerald Hiestand (Eds.) *Becoming a Pastor Theologian: New Possibilities for Church Leadership*. InterVarsity Press. 2016. (pp. 8 - 24).

God and teach things which are contrary to it. And therein lies the test of false teaching. If what is said is contrary to what the Scriptures say, it is false teaching.

Pastor theologians must be relevant. That is the role Christian missionaries have always had. They have to learn the culture in order to preach the gospel in a way the people will understand. This is what pastor theologians in Western culture must also do. But in understanding our culture we do not compromise the truth of the gospel because of a false belief we are making it more acceptable. The pastor theologian must understand Western culture and preach gospel truth into it in a way it understands. It may not like what it hears but the pastor theologian resists the temptation to preach another gospel. Not that there is another gospel (see Galatians 1:6 – 8).

The pastor theologian's task in understanding Western culture and how to preach into it is with the purpose of equipping the saints to build the body of Christ. Part of the task is to help God's people to understand liberal theology so they can see its errors. The task is to help people have confidence in the Scriptures so they are not taken captive by the wolves and false teachers.

In this chapter I have encouraged pastors to be theologians, for being a theologian is essential to the task of being a pastor. I have also encouraged pastors to pay attention to the process people are going through when we draw alongside to offer pastoral care. Getting this balance right is a difficult task. To do it well I have also encouraged pastors to make sure they are having regular pastoral supervision to help reflect on their pastoral practice and how they are doing at integrating being a pastoral theologian with interacting with people in a messy world.

In the next chapter I address some fuzzy thinking about pastoral ministry and talk about what the role of the pastor teacher is not. I see the role of the pastor teacher as essential to Christian mission in the world. Calls, therefore, to declericalise the church are wrong calls, and I try to explain why I think so in the next chapter.

3

WHAT IS PASTORAL CARE?

PASTORAL CARE AND THE PRIESTHOOD OF ALL BELIEVERS.

In the introduction, I made the point that pastors need formal theological education so that they can exercise their responsibilities as pastoral carers. Some reading this book will find this idea a bit disturbing. Surely a person who doesn't have a theological education can be a pastoral carer? Emphasising the doctrine of the *Priesthood of all believers*, some Christians insist that pastoral ministry is not limited to ordained pastors but that every believer has a ministry.

I want to shout fervent agreement with the idea that ministry is not limited to those who are ordained. To say that only those who are ordained can exercise ministry is to fly in the face of Paul's teaching in Ephesians 4:12. It is *the saints*[19] who do the work of ministry. It is the role of every

---

19   In context, the saints referred to in Paul's letter to the Ephesians are not a special class of Christians. Paul refers to all Christians when he uses the term *saints*. All Christians, in the Apostle's thinking, are a special class because all Christians are in Christ. If you are a Christian, you are a saint.

Christian person to do the work of ministry. It is the role of pastor teachers to equip the saints to do this. This role of pastor teachers, to equip the saints for ministry, is pastoral care. But it is not the role of every Christian to engage in pastoral ministry, the ministry of pastor teachers.

The error I see in linking the distinctive of the priesthood of all believers with the ministry of the pastor teacher, is that this is not really the biblical teaching of the apostle Peter who introduces the idea of the priesthood of all believers. The idea of the priesthood of all believers comes from Peter's teaching in 1 Peter 2. In verse 5, Peter says, "you yourselves like living stones are being built up as a spiritual house, to be a holy priesthood, to offer spiritual sacrifices acceptable to God through Jesus Christ" (ESV). Again, in verse 9 Peter says, "But you are a chosen race, a royal priesthood, a holy nation, a people for his own possession, that you may proclaim the excellencies of him who called you out of darkness into his marvellous light" (ESV). This role is confirmed by the apostle John in Revelation 5:9 – 10.

Looking at the role of priest with a biblical theology perspective, the distinctiveness of the priestly function is that a priest has the privilege and responsibility to represent the people of God in the presence of God. When the Levitical priesthood was established, its purpose was to offer sacrifice on behalf of the people (see Exodus 29:38 – 44; Leviticus 6:12; 24:5 – 9; Numbers 10:1 – 10). In order to offer sacrifice the priest had to enter the presence of God in the holy place. Only a priest was allowed to enter the presence of God. That is the distinctive of priesthood: Entering the presence of God. That's why Peter says that Christians are now a *holy priesthood*. All Christians have the privilege of entering the presence of God because Christ, our High Priest, has gone before us. He has opened the way. He has gone into the Holy of holies and made a way for us to enter. All Christians have the privilege and honour of entering the presence of God. We are all priests.

Having the privilege to enter God's presence doesn't mean all the saints can therefore do the same ministry as a pastor teacher, or an apostle, or a prophet, or an evangelist. These are distinctive ministries given to distinctive people which together, according to Ephesians 4:11, form one gift. This one gift of God, which has been given to each of us (Eph. 4:7), is God's way of equipping all of us for the work of ministry.

Having the privilege to enter God's presence also does not mean we just go in and then do nothing. Peter explains the purpose of entering God's presence is for us to proclaim the excellencies of God (1 Peter 2:9). To whom or what do we proclaim how excellent our God is? To the universe! To every created being. Peter has already explained that our salvation is something into which angels long to look (1 Peter 1:12). The image in 1 Peter 1:12 is as though, when the Holy Spirit was working on us, to convince us of the truth of the gospel, there were the angels in heaven, straining to see, excitedly pushing each other out of the way so to speak, to see if we had finally come to understand that Jesus is Lord. When we finally said, "Yes. Jesus is my Lord!", and came into the presence of God, we, now as a royal priesthood, proclaim the excellencies of God to all those angels who were barracking for us.

For every Christian as a priest, we have the privilege of entering God's presence and of joining in the chorus of praise to God. It also means that every Christian has unfettered access to the word of God. The doctrine of the *Priesthood of all Believers* means we do not recognise a caste of believers who have exclusive authority to read and to teach the Scriptures. There is no exclusive group of Christians who exercise God's role of forgiveness. But according to Ephesians 4:11 God has given distinctive ministries in the church, and they are not open to every believer.

As I have said above, I agree with the idea that ministry is not limited to those who are ordained. Ministry is not even limited to those who are theologically trained. It is the saints, the people of God, who do the work of ministry. This is clear in Eph. 4:12. God has given the saints a gift to equip them for their ministry. That gift is apostles, prophets, evangelists, pastors and teachers. It is not the priesthood of all believers that enables Christians to be equipped for ministry. It is the ministry of apostles, prophets, evangelists, pastors and teachers that equips God's people for ministry. I don't mean that every Christian is an apostle, prophet, evangelist or pastor teacher. What I do mean is that that group of ministries has been given by God to each of us to equip us for the work of ministry. That group of ministries is God's one gift which equips us for ministry. If I want to work out what ministry I have in the congregation I will listen to what my pastor teacher says, and I will listen to the apostles, prophets and evangelists (I will read the Bible). By this gift of God to me I will be equipped for ministry, the building of the body of Christ.

I want to challenge the idea that the priesthood of all believers means that any Christian can do the work of a pastor teacher. Rather, I want to suggest that just as not every Christian is an apostle, prophet or evangelist, not every Christian is a pastor teacher. The Christian doctrine of the priesthood of all believers has nothing to do with ministry. It is a doctrine about status. The status of a Christian is that we are in heaven, in the presence of God, and therefore we are priests. As such we proclaim His glory. In a rather provocatively titled article Timothy Wengert says, "the common understanding of "the priesthood of all believers" cannot mean, "anyone can be a pastor", but rather, "all of us are members of the one Body of Christ and individually servants to each other in our respective offices."[20]

This means every Christian has a ministry of proclaiming the glory of God. We have this ministry by the privilege of our status as priests who enter the presence of God. But we are not all pastors. It is the ministry of apostles, prophets, evangelists, pastors and teachers which equips us for the ministry of declaring to the universe, the glory of God.

EQUIPPED TO BUILD THE BODY

I have argued earlier that the essence of ordained ministry is pastoral care. This means I am also arguing that not every Christian can do pastoral care. By this rather radical statement, I do not mean the majority of Christians shouldn't care about other people. On the contrary. We know the salvation of God. How can we not care about and for people who are lost in their sin and alienated from God? When we see the poor and marginalised, how can we not care, because we ourselves were once lost and without hope in this world? Of course, Christians care for people. What I am arguing for is that pastoral care is such a distinctive element of ordained ministry, we must maintain its distinctiveness and not confuse it with other forms of ministry. Secular thought has "professionalised" pastoral care and given it to psychologists, counsellors, and aid organisations. Christians have accepted this professionalising, and this has resulted in side-lining the pastor teacher.

---

[20] Timothy J. Wengert, "The Priesthood of All Believers and Other Pious Myths," Institute of Liturgical Studies Occasional Papers. Paper 117 (2006). 11

In arguing that pastoral care is a distinctive ministry of the ordained, and therefore theologically trained, pastor, I am not arguing for a hierarchy of believers. I am not saying that pastor teachers are superior Christians. In Christ there is no distinction. There is neither Jew nor Greek, slave nor free. There is not male and female (see Galatians 3:28). All believers are equal in Christ. This is the idea behind the doctrine of the priesthood of all believers. We all, without distinction, have the freedom to enter the presence of God.

Some see *declericalisation* as essential to the mission of the church in the 21st century. I am, in fact, arguing the opposite. It is my contention in this book that we need to reconnect with the essence of pastoral ministry. We need to make sure the pastor teacher is doing the work of the pastor teacher. We need to make sure the role of the ordained minister is seen as distinct from other ministries that the saints do. According to Eph. 4:12 it is the role of our pastors to equip the saints. If we declericalise pastoral ministry, we are saying to our pastor teachers, "Don't equip us for ministry." How can we say that to our pastors when God says to us this is their role?

The problem with teaching that the priesthood of all believers means that all believers can do the same work as our pastors, because we are all equal, is highlighted here. When the apostle Paul describes the gifts that God has given to the body of Christ he asks, "Are all apostles? Are all prophets? Are all teachers? Do all work miracles? Do all possess gifts of healing? Do all speak with tongues? Do all interpret?" (1 Corinthians 12:29 – 30). The implied answer to these questions is, "No. Not all Christians are apostles, or prophets or teachers etc." Paul points out there are differences in the body of Christ for the benefit of the whole.

In one sense, we must *reclericalise* the church, not declericalise it. We must get back to the idea that the distinctive of ordained Christian ministry is the *cure of souls*. Such ministry is essential to the body of Christ. Declericalisation promotes the idea that pastoral care is not important. Pastoral care is not the exclusive domain of pastor teachers, but it is at the core of their role. You can't have a pastor teacher who does not exercise pastoral care. And you cannot have saints equipped for ministry without pastor teachers exercising their ministry. To equip the saints, we must have clergy (pastor teachers) being clerical (equipping the saints).

It is more than likely that because the secular idea of pastoral care has infiltrated Christian thinking, we have come to believe anybody who is caring (and that's every Christian, right?) can do pastoral care. If, therefore, everybody can do pastoral care, the body of Christ no longer has need of pastor teachers. We can therefore declericalise the church. This is the danger of taking our lead from secular society. Non-biblical beliefs turn Christian ideals on their heads.

THE PASTORAL CARE SETTING

Modern, western thinking is that pastoral care is something that happens in a crisis situation. The idea is that it is only in situations of addiction to drugs, homelessness, unemployment, trouble with the law, financial problems, mental health issues, relationship conflict etc. that pastoral care becomes necessary. Of course, pastoral care is needed in these situations, but the modern, secular idea is that it is needed only in these crisis type situations. In reality, pastoral care is something that is needed in the whole of life. Pastoral care equips people for life even when they are not facing a crisis. Pastoral care that focuses on the whole of life is pastoral care that will help people avoid crisis situations. Whole of life pastoral care will equip the saints to live in the world with a decidedly Christian focus.

The focus of the pastor teacher's pastoral care of God's people is to equip the saints for ministry. This ministry of the saints is to build the body of Christ. What this looks like in practical terms is that the body of Christ will be a functioning community. It will be a community that build's itself in love. God's people will love being part of this community because of the loving support it provides. The joy of belonging to the body of Christ is a foretaste of heaven. Who wouldn't want to be part of such a community?

The Christian community will build itself in love when every member is working properly (Ephesians 4:16), that is, when every member is exercising their ministry. This is what pastoral care is all about. It ultimately builds Christian community. Pastor teachers need to focus their ministry on how to equip the saints, so this community of Christ is built.

This is what congregations are asking their pastors when they ask them to get Sunday right. Getting Sunday right is speaking to, encouraging and equipping people to be Christian in their secular world. It is helping Christians to be Christian in the workplace, in the playground, at the basketball match and, yes, even at the pub. Getting Sunday right is such an important topic it is discussed fully in Chapter Six.

EQUIPPED TO LIVE IN THE WORLD

Most of what the secular Western world proclaims as tolerance is just another version of the Emperor's New Clothes. The story of the Emperor's New Clothes was written in 1837 by Hans Christian Andersen, a Danish writer of children's fairy tales. In short, the story tells of an emperor whose vanity led him to be deceived by a couple of charlatans who proclaimed they could make him the most glorious outfit from very special material that only they could weave. So special was this material that only true connoisseurs of the fine things of life could actually see it. To others, it was simply invisible. Of course, there was nothing to see. The weavers took the emperor's money and fled. In the meantime, the emperor paraded in the streets in his fine new clothes. Everybody admired them, not willing to let on that they were the only ones whose lack of appreciation of the fine things of life meant they could not see the emperor's new clothes. It was not until a young child in the crowd, in childish innocence, yelled out, "the emperor has no clothes," that the people came to their senses and realised it was true. There was nothing to see except the emperor parading in the streets in his underwear.

It takes a lot of courage, or simple childish innocence, to speak against the flow of political correctness in today's Western society. Christians know how to live in God's world, because God has told us. We have the Bible to tell us how men and women should relate to each other. We have the Bible to tell us how parents should treat their children. We have the Bible to tell us how a Christian should behave in the workplace. The Bible teaches us the value of life created in the image of God. It teaches us to care for the weak, marginalised, and vulnerable. The Bible teaches us the value of God's creation and therefore how to tend and care for the environment.

Western secularism is following another path. Western secularism has come to the point of believing that human identity is in the individual rather than in the image of God. Not only does this individualism touch on the area of sexual identity and practice but it also impacts on the vulnerability of the unborn, the sick and elderly.

In many places in the western world Christians have not been able to stand against this tide flowing away from God's word. This is where Christian pastoral care comes in. This is where Christian pastors stand up and speak out to God's people about how to live in this modern secular world. This is where pastors remind God's people that while we live in this world, we are not of this world. We have a different standard to the values of modern Western morality.

The early Christians did it. They brought a Christian morality to bear on a secular world that did not value the life of the vulnerable person. They rescued the unwanted baby from the rubbish tip where it had been thrown. They brought the vulnerable widow, in a society that did not provide a social security net, into the protection of those who had more of the world's goods. The fourth century Roman Emperor Julian, complained about Christian behaviour because, in his estimation, it turned people away from the Roman gods. He said, "Atheism[21] has been especially advanced through the loving service rendered to strangers, and through their care for the burial of the dead. It is a scandal that there is not a single Jew who is a beggar, and that the godless Galileans[22] care not only for their own poor but for ours as well; while those who belong to us look in vain for the help that we should render them."

---

21 This is the word Emperor Julian used for Christians and Jews because they did not have idols in the synagogue or other places where they gathered. Without an idol they did not have a god to worship when they met together.
22 "godless Galileans" are the Christians. They have no gods (no idols) and follow the man from Galilee.

Why was it that the Christians of the fourth century were noted for their acts of charity, for their care of the vulnerable? It was because their pastor teachers were getting Sunday right. Pastor teachers were showing pastoral care of the people of God by teaching them the things of God. The people then went out during the week and lived the Christian life in their communities. They took the message of the gospel into the public square and showed a secular world how God expects us to live.

When the Old Testament prophets spoke words of criticism and judgement against God's own people it was because the people of God had forgotten their relationship with God. They had forgotten what their God had done for them. The people of God had forgotten that their God had rescued them from slavery and brought them into a land flowing with milk and honey.

Take, for example, what the prophet Amos said to the people of Israel. In Amos 4:1, Amos calls the women, "cows of Basham". This is a great insult. But Amos has pointed out that these women are lazing around like well fed cattle while they oppress the poor and crush the needy. So luxurious was their lifestyle they simply ordered their husbands so they might drink together. It is a scene of indulgent luxury while they subjugate others in desperate need. These women, wallowing in extravagance, are those whom God rescued from slavery in Egypt (see Amos 3:1). Surely, they, of all people, should have had compassion on the poor and needy. Surely, as God's own people, whom God rescued from slavery, these women and their husbands would be so thankful to God for their undeserved relationship with Him, that they would share their material wealth with those in need.

This is the sort of Christian teaching the pastor teachers of the fourth century were sharing with God's flock when Emperor Julian complained about their loving care for others. Those Christians were well aware of the amazing and undeserved grace of God in their lives. They were well aware that God had rescued them from idolatry. They had turned to God from idols to serve the living and true God (1 Thessalonians 1:9). They were well aware that Jesus had paid the ultimate price for their sin. They did not indulge themselves but reached out to those in need to exhibit something of the grace of God to the poor and oppressed.

Many years ago, Donald Browning wrote, "Pastoral care is the more or less unstructured general work with youths, couples, adults and other such groups in various types of informal and formal conversations, dialogues, and other communicative interactions. Pastoral care in this sense occurs on the street corner, at the end of the committee meeting, in the hospital room, in and around the funeral, and in many other more or less marginal situations."[23] I want to agree with the idea that pastoral care is general work with God's people. I want to say it is the essence of pastoral ministry. However, I want to disagree with the idea that it happens in, "more or less marginal situations", if he means that "marginal situations" are the only places where pastoral care takes place. I want to say that pastoral care takes place everywhere. It happens in the mainstream situations as well as the marginal situations. If pastor teachers are doing their job, pastoral care is always happening. Pastoral care defines the role of the pastor teacher.

Pastoral care does not just take care of people in crisis situations. Pastoral

---

23 Donald S. Browning, "Introduction to Pastoral Counselling" in *Clinical Handbook of Pastoral Counselling*, Volume 1, Expanded Edition, ed. Robert J. Wicks, Richard D. Parsons, Donald Capps, Mahwah, (New Jersey: Paulist Press, 1985), 5-13.

care equips the saints for the work of ministry (Ephesians. 4:12). Pastoral care teaches God's people how to build the body of Christ so they can live God's way in a secular world. It teaches them how to take the gospel of the Lord Jesus Christ into the public square and so disturb the culture of the day that even the Emperor complains about it. Pastoral care reminds the people of God that they were once slaves in Egypt and calls on them to care for the poor and oppressed.

The real distinctive in Christian pastoral care is that it is not this world focused. Christian pastoral care recognises that men and women are created in the image of God. This means that we are each a valued person. In saying that, I am not saying that as a person I can be whoever I want to be. I am a person, male or female, created in God's image. My identity as a person is in God or, more specifically, in Christ. My identity is not in my sexual orientation, or in my job, my ethnicity, wealth, the suburb in which I live, or in who I choose to be. As a Christian, my identity is in Christ.

Now, someone is yelling in my ear that in Christ there is neither male nor female! Galatians 3:28 says, "there is no male and female … in Christ". In this passage Paul is talking about unity in Christ. Everybody in Christ is justified by faith. We are all sons of God through faith. Yes, we are all sons, male and female. We are all sons because the way the New Testament uses this word is in the sense of *first-born*. It is the first-born son who inherits the family wealth. Every Christian is a *first-born son*. All of us inherit the wealth of God. We have all put on Christ. Everybody. There's no distinction in Christ. There's no Jew nor Greek, slave nor free, male and female. We are all united in Christ irrespective of our position in life (see Galatians 3:23 – 28). We are all sons of God.

Maybe it would be better to translate the idea that all Christians, male and female, are sons of God, with dynamic equivalence rather than word for word. Instead of reading that we are "sons of God", and thereby alienating half the population who regard such statements as sexist, the translation would read, we are "first born of God". I don't believe such a translation is capitulating to 21st century secular ideas of political correctness. If the gospel tells men and women they are both "first born of God", it doesn't sound like a very good idea to tell them they are "sons of God". If we use this word for word translation, we still have to explain it, as I did above. Why then not use a dynamic equivalence translation that immediately speaks to all people that, in Christ, we all have the privileges of the first born? In Christ, we all inherit the Kingdom of God. But I am distracted. We were discussing the nature of humanity.

Contrary to modern Western secular thought, all people are the image of God. That is our identity. Black or white, abled or disabled, mentally disturbed or in our right mind, still in the womb or at the end of life, all are the image of God. Secular Western thought has struggled with human identity among obvious diversity. It has struggled hard and has come up with some solutions. What I am suggesting is that those solutions are the wrong solutions because they emphasise the right of the individual while ignoring the person we are under God. This is what I mean about the Emperor's New Clothes. Too many Christians have followed Western secular thinking and cannot see the reality in front of them. Christians need to stand for Christian values, not change our values because some charlatans have convinced us of a different reality. In the light of what the Bible teaches us, the naked propaganda of modern Western values is exposed before us.

Here I am not suggesting Christians should impose Christian values on a secular world. It is sad to see Western culture changing and rejecting Christian values it once held to. But it is not for us to impose Christian morality on unbelievers. That is pure legalism. The Christians of Emperor Julian's day didn't impose Christian morality on non-Christians. They also did not accept the values and morality of the world around them. They had discovered a better way. They did not live the Christian life in a quiet little corner. They engaged with the world of their day. They went into the world and where they saw non-Christian values, they brought a Christian presence and Christian behaviour. They simply lived the Christian life and changed the world.

A short while ago I saw a post on Face Book that suggested when caring for the frail elderly, we should keep in mind who they once were. The frail lady in room 9, who now can't remember her family members when they come to visit, was once a schoolteacher or a nurse or a company executive. The suggestion in the post was that this woman should be treated well for who she once was. While it is a good thing to remember that the person we might meet for the first time in their frail old age, once made a valued contribution to society and has family who have been blessed by them, their identity as a person does not derive from any of these. Rather, they are a person created in the image of God and they still bear that image today. Their dementia has not diminished God's image. They are still very much remembered and loved by God. This is the reason we care for people. Our identity is in God, not in who we are or what we do, nor in who we once were and once did.

Recognising all humanity is created in the image of God (Genesis 1:27) is the basis of pastoral care. The respect we give a person is not in what they used to be nor in what they may be. We do not care for our fellow human beings for the potential they may have to be someone better (whatever being "better" might mean). We care for each other simply because we are all created in the image of God.

A friend of mine retired after a lifetime of work as a successful businessman. He didn't want to sit around doing nothing so went to his local neighbourhood centre to volunteer. The centre had a mentoring program where volunteers were matched with clients who found life difficult and lacked normal social skills. My friend spent some time with a young man, meeting together once or twice a week. After a few months my friend gave up volunteering because he said it was impossible to change the young man he had been matched with. And therein lies the problem. The purpose of my friend's role as a mentor was not to change the young man. Changing another person is never anyone's role. My friend did not see this young man as a person created in the image of God, but as a "project" to improve.

Believing that a fellow human being is someone I can help to "improve" or someone who used to be a "valuable" member of society, is to assign to them a status lower than that which they in fact have. We must stop assessing people by enlightenment and economic terms. A person's "value" is not in how much they contribute to society. We might be able to improve a person's situation by providing housing, food, medical care etc. But we can't "improve" them. They are a person for whom Christ died. What is there to improve? Being a human, being in the image of God, is the greatest status we have. To look for something else to assign "value" to in a person is to diminish them as a person. In pastoral care we come alongside the other as the image of God. I think this is why just being with another person is so powerful. As a fellow human draws alongside me, I draw near to the image of God and I am reminded of who I am, also the image of God.

I am not suggesting that it is always easy to draw alongside another. We all have our prejudices and find some people difficult. We probably need to examine ourselves fairly closely to understand these prejudices and to change who we are. But there remains a difficulty for a lot of pastors when we deal with sinful people. Of course, we remember that we are sinful people ourselves, but there are some sins which we find so disturbing that we just don't know how to deal with them in others. We can end up just laying down the law. "Stop it!" we say. That's usually not very supportive nor effective.

Some years ago, I was asked to consider a position as a prison chaplain. My immediate thought was, "No thank you. I couldn't minister to *those* people." At the time I was volunteering in our church outreach café. Our church was in the red-light district of our city and the café was in a seedy back lane. As I reflected on my reaction to the offer of becoming a prison chaplain, I realised that half our clientele in the café had just come out of prison, and the other half were just about to go to prison. I realised "those people" were ordinary people with the same hopes and dreams all of us have. "Those people" were ordinary people created in the image of God.

When I finally became a prison chaplain, I encountered a number of paedophiles. I found most of them difficult to speak with. Some continued their predatory behaviour in prison, seeking to abuse the younger, more vulnerable, inmates. It is hard to see the image of God in such people. But it is there. It takes a long and patient time of *being alongside* to see this image slowly shine through. It is not an easy task.

I said above that pastoral care is not about changing a person. You may ask that if it is not about changing people, then, what is pastoral care about? Pastoral care is about *being*. A person may require help and we can often offer a hand up which will improve their circumstances. But our goal is never to *rescue* a person. They have one rescuer and that is Jesus Christ. Our goal in pastoral care is always to draw alongside, to offer comfort and encouragement. Our goal is to encourage the other to understand *how* God is with them in their situation. Pastoral care desires the other to be who they are, the image of God. Even the paedophile, as they begin to catch glimpses of the image of God in themselves and in their victims, can begin to see something of the evil of their predatory behaviour.

Coming alongside another to offer comfort and encouragement is never to give the impression that sinful behaviour is OK. It is not OK to abuse children. It is not OK to be a glutton. Coming alongside will often encourage the person who is aware of their sin to confess it to God and seek His strength to defeat it. Where a person is not aware of their sin, or even believes what they have done is not sinful, the work of pastoral care is harder. I was once talking with a young man who was fully aware of his sexual sin. As his pastor I tried to communicate acceptance of him as a person in the image of God. He responded to me by saying that he felt I was saying, "Accept the sinner, but not the sin." This was a problem for him because he believed his sexual behaviour was very much a part of his identity, if not his whole identity. His belief was therefore that I could not accept him as a person without accepting his sexual behaviour.

Pastoral care works alongside to encourage a person to know their identity as the image of God. Sometimes we encounter those who refuse to accept this identity and insist they are their own master. Let's face it, all of us have difficulty living as the image of God. We struggle to live the way God wants us to live. We find we have particular sinful behaviour that is besetting. But for none of us is this an excuse for sin. For those who desire to live as God's person, pastoral care will keep on encouraging them to live as the image of God. For those who refuse to live under the Lordship of Christ, our task is to clearly, lovingly, pastorally, present the gospel. It is silly to try to make someone who does not know Jesus as Lord to obey his commandments. That speaks of salvation by works. We do not want people thinking they can be saved by a change in lifestyle. We want people to know the loving grace of God and to be saved by grace through faith alone.

To return to the young man who thought it was impossible for me to accept him as a person because I could not accept his sexual behaviour. He believed his sexual orientation and behaviour gave him identity. As a Christian, I believe our identity is in Christ and that every human is created in the image of God. While the young man was right that I couldn't accept his sinful behaviour, I believe he was wrong that I couldn't accept him as a person because, in reality, his identity is not in sexual orientation or behaviour. He has a mistaken idea of where human identity lies. Here we have two world views in collision. It is my job as a Christian not to shout across the divide but to encourage him to catch a glimpse of the image of God in himself.

It is possible for Christians to have friendship with those whose lifestyle we disagree with. While some of them may think we cannot accept them as a person unless we accept their lifestyle, my experience is that most of my non-Christian friends know the Christian ethics I live by, and we still enjoy good friendship. We are able to have civil conversations. We are able to debate political and other issues of the day. We have lunch together. We enjoy each other's company. They know I do not agree with some of their behaviours, even behaviour by which they identify themselves as a person. But this does not interfere with our friendships. It is often these friends who will come to me at times of difficulty when they struggle with life.

I value these friendships and I do not see them simply as an opportunity to preach the gospel. I long for my friends to know Jesus and I pray regularly for them. I will take opportunities to encourage them to know Jesus, especially those times they come to me for help. I value these friendships for what they are. These friends are people like me. We may have the same sense of humour. We may have the same interests. I love sailing and have a lot of sailing friends who don't know Jesus, but we have great conversations about sailing. We can use all the jargon without having to explain to a non-sailor what we're talking about. We relax in these conversations. We feel comfortable in each other's company. We are refreshed.

What has this got to do with pastoral care? It is the pastoral care I receive from my pastor teacher that equips me to have these friends and these conversations. I am not in crisis, but my pastor teacher gives me pastoral care every Sunday. He comes alongside me both in his preaching and in the casual conversations we have. He knows my life, the work I do and the things I enjoy. His ministry equips me for ministry in the world. Yes, I am an academic and I teach pastoral care. I know all about it! I write books about it. But I need pastoral care. I need daily reminding of who I am in Christ. I need pastoral care that will equip me for ministry in the church and in the world.

CONCLUSION

Pastoral care that equips us for ministry in the church and in the world is pastoral care that will aid us to avoid crisis situations. If a crisis happens, the regular pastoral care we have been receiving will have already equipped us to face the crisis. I am not suggesting that where God's people receive regular whole-of-life pastoral care, they will never face a crisis. Life is messy and things get messed up. We get an unexpected negative health diagnosis. A child is killed in a car crash. The family breadwinner is told by their boss that their position has been made redundant. The unexpected happens and throws our lives into crisis. Whole of life pastoral care will help to lessen the impact of the unexpected crisis. We will be better equipped to handle a crisis if we have been constantly cared for by whole-of-life pastoral care. Also, because we belong to the Body of Christ, we belong to a community which builds itself in love. When we face crises, we will have that loving support around us.

In this chapter I have talked about what pastoral ministry is not and have encouraged you, in your pastoral practice, to relate to people as persons created in the image of God. Our pastoral conversations are an attempt to help people understand this is who they are. As you might expect, one thing Western secular thought misses out on is an understanding of God and how He relates to people. Christian pastoral care seeks to express the character of God as we interact with our fellow human beings. The next chapter looks carefully at expressing the character of God in pastoral care.

4

EXPRESSING THE CHARACTER OF GOD IN PASTORAL CARE.

GOD'S FELLOWSHIP WITH HUMANITY

When God created the world, His essential purpose was to be in fellowship with His people. The world was created through and for the Son (Colossians 1:16). The creation was the Father's gift to the Son. When God created humanity as the pinnacle of the whole created order, it was for fellowship. God walked in the garden in fellowship with humanity (Genesis 3:8.)

Creating humanity as His agent to care for and delight in creation (Genesis 1:28 – 29) was God's essential purpose because fellowship is in His essential nature. God Himself is in eternal fellowship with Himself. As the Father loves the Son, so He loves the Spirit. As the Son loves the Father, he also loves the Spirit. As the Holy Spirit loves the Father, he also loves the Son. This is the nature of God. God is love (1 John 4:8, 16). This love works itself out in fellowship. In creating humanity as His agent,

God has created humanity to be in loving fellowship with Himself.

The Bible expresses, in a number of places, God's love for humanity. God created humanity to be His agent in the world, to look after and to care for the creation (Genesis 2:15). God was present with mankind in this garden (Genesis 3:8). The Psalmist wonders at how and why the God who created the heavens and the earth should care about [apparently] insignificant human beings (Palms. 8:3 – 4, 144:1 – 3). Jesus came to serve us, not to be served by us (Mark 10:45). These passages show God's desire to be with His people and express His love toward us. John 3:16 tells us that God's motivation in giving His Son was His love for us. The outcome of God's love is that those who believe will be in eternal fellowship with God. They shall not die but have everlasting life (John 6:40, 47 – 51).

Pastoral care takes its lead from God. As God becomes one of us and lives among us (John 1:14), He is among us as our servant (John 13:13 – 15). Being our servant is an expression of God's love for us. And God's love leads us into eternal fellowship. While the act of creating the universe was an act of love, this love of God has reached out to us especially now that we are in crisis, separated and alienated from God. When we were still sinners Christ died for us (Romans 5:8). What greater crisis can humanity be in other than that we are sinners, people estranged from and at enmity with God? It was in this condition, with no hope and without God in the world (Ephesians 2:12), that God reached out to us.

Pastoral care is not just about helping people in crisis. Pastoral care is not only about helping people in grief at the death of a loved one. It's not only about helping people who have experienced a life-threatening injury or health scare. Pastoral care is not just about being there for people who are going through a relationship breakdown. Christian pastoral care is more than just helping people through some crisis event that is making it difficult for them to get on with life. *Pastoral care is the core of pastoral ministry.* Pastoral care goes beyond helping a person to get on with life. Pastoral care is the core of pastoral ministry because it deals with the greatest crisis humanity faces, our estrangement from God. And the goal of pastoral care is to bring people back into relationship with God. It is true to say that in our disobedience our relationship has been broken. But it is not ended. Expressing His love towards us, God keeps on coming back at us. He keeps on encouraging us to know the love He has for us. He wants us to be in full fellowship with Him.

We need to understand that a crisis in our life does not end our relationship with God. The primary task of pastoral care is to help the other person to see how God is with them, even in their crisis. When Job had lost all, his wife gave him the silly advice to curse God and die (Job 2:9). The loss of all his children and his health was enough for Job's wife to suggest that euthanasia or suicide was a sensible solution to his situation. In his response to his wife, Job recognised that God is God. If we accept the good from him, we should also be prepared to accept the bad (Job 2:10).

At the onset of his troubles Job at least understood that God is God and we therefore worship Him whatever He sends our way. Job did not understand what was happening to him. He agreed with most of the unsolicited advice that came his way, but he insisted he had done nothing wrong and couldn't understand why God had sent all this calamity on him. It was not until Job finally came to know God that things turned around for him (Job 42:5 – 6). Job came to understand that through it all God had been with him. He needed to come to understand *how* God was present, not *why* things had turned out the way they had.

For a pastor teacher, the goal of pastoral care is not to help a person to get through their crisis. The goal of pastoral care is to encourage people to know God's peace. Pastoral care will help people to know that peace of God in the whole of life as well as in the middle of crisis. While it might be our hope that we can support a person through a crisis situation until the crisis passes, this is not our goal.

When Jesus stood among his disciples in the locked room on the evening of the day he rose from the dead, he declared peace to be with them (John 20:19). Immediately after declaring peace, he showed them his hands and his side. The marks of his torturous death were still present. While Jesus had been raised from the dead, the marks of his pain were still visible, at the same time he declared peace to his disciples. The peace of God and the signs of torture and death were present together in that same moment. And yet it was these marks of death, indeed the death itself, which has brought reconciliation between humanity and God. The relationship that had been broken by sin has now been restored by the blood of Jesus.

While fellowship with God is now possible for all humanity, we continue with the scars of sin which still distract and harm, but we are comforted by the peace of Christ breathed into us while he still bore the marks of his agony and distress. Christian pastoral care enables us to live the whole of life and also even in crisis, with the peace of God. The peace of God may deliver us from crisis, but this is not its aim. The peace of God enables us to live in God's peace no matter our circumstances. Our pain may remain, our scars may still be visible, but God's peace is also present.

I was once ministering to a woman who had MS. Multiple Sclerosis is a disease of the central nervous system where the immune system attacks the protective sheath (myelin) that covers nerve fibres in the body. The disease causes communication problems between the brain and the rest of the body. Eventually, the disease can cause permanent damage or deterioration of the nerves. Elaine's condition had deteriorated to the point where she was no longer able to walk. She was bed ridden and needed daily help. Elaine loved the Lord Jesus and I often found she ministered more to me than I to her. I said to her one day that I was sorry that she was in her current situation. She responded that she was quite happy because the Lord was with her. Elaine had learned that the peace of God, which passes all understanding, was keeping her heart and mind in the knowledge and love of God and of His Son, Jesus Christ our Lord. Elaine was truly blessed. Her "crisis" paled into insignificance in the light of her relationship with God. The peace that had come to her when she was reconciled with God overwhelmed her deteriorating body. The greater peace of being in fellowship with the God of love was far more real and satisfying than any temporary peace a remission of her MS might have brought her.

God's desire is to have His people eternally with Him. His desire is for fellowship with those whom He has chosen. To express the character of God in pastoral care we express the desire to have fellowship with God's people including those in crisis. Or rather, our aim is that others may be in fellowship with us and with God. That is, that they may know they are not alone in life or in crisis. Our aim in pastoral care is that the person we are ministering to may know that in their life they have the support, understanding and care of their fellow human beings even if they are in distress. Ultimately, our hope is that the pastoral care we offer allows people to know that God has not abandoned them, but His peace remains with them in all of life. Elaine, even in her distress, had understood this.

When in crisis, many people ask the question, "Why?" "Why is God doing this?" or "Why does God allow this to happen to me?" "Why doesn't God do something to make this better?" There is no easy answer to this question of "why". There is a theological answer which has to do with original sin and the fact that the creation groans as in pains of childbirth (see Romans 8:18 – 22), but this is rarely a satisfying answer to a personal crisis. The question remains of why this crisis might be happening to me and not to someone else. As the Psalmist laments, some ask why the wicked prosper (see Psalm 73:1 – 13).

A better question to seek an answer to in life, and especially in the middle of crisis, is the question of, "How?" "How is God in this?" "How is God with me in life or in this crisis?" Elaine had discovered the answer to this question and her critical health situation became much less important to her than her relationship with God. If we feel God is distant in life or even has abandoned us, we know there is nothing in our experience that Christ has not also experienced (Hebrews 4:15). Jesus even experienced being abandoned by the Father (Mark 15:34). And yet, at his darkest hour, he was raised to life, being restored to fellowship with his Father.

I have found, when helping people in crisis to put life into perspective, a simple technique to focus on God in the midst of crisis. I suggest as you read this technique, you actually do it also. This way you will feel some of the power it has to help in a time of crisis. Cup your hands in front of you, as though you are holding something and intently looking at it. Imagine what you are holding is the crisis facing you. As you stare at it, it fills your whole vision. The area outside your hands even goes out of focus. This is what happens when a crisis fills your life. It becomes the only thing you can see. It is hardly possible to see anything else let alone a solution or way forward.

Now, still holding your hands where they are, with your crisis filling your vision, lift your eyes. Don't move your hands. Look up and see what is beyond your hands. Take in the scene. Let your vision focus on what is around you. If you have kept your hands still, with your crisis cupped in them, you realise your crisis has taken on a different perspective. As you have raised your eyes and taken in what is beyond you, your crisis has shrunk with your new perspective. Then, look up. Look right up into the sky. If you're indoors, image you are looking through the roof. Image it disappears and you are looking into the sky. Keep staring at the sky and see how big the universe is. Ponder the magnificence of God and His majestic beauty. If you have kept your hands in place, still holding your crisis, you will realise, as you have been contemplating the beauty of God's creation and the glory of the God who made it, your crisis has almost disappeared. It has become so tiny it is almost insignificant. In fact, your crisis hasn't changed at all. What has changed is your perspective on life.

This little exercise is a simple technique to help put life in perspective. It helps to begin to understand *how* God is with me in my crisis. He is so much bigger, so much more majestic than anything I face in the messiness of life. My crisis becomes so tiny it almost disappears and God fills me and everything around me.

The Christian can be assured that God is with them (Matthew 28:20). If that is true, then a person needs to understand *how* God is with them, even in a crisis situation, even when they might feel God has abandoned them.

As a chaplain in hospitals and prisons I was given the amazing privilege on many occasions of being invited into a person's life as they shared with me the joys and challenges of their experiences over many years. Often these were things their close friends and even intimate family had not known about. I would often hear the words, "I've never told anyone this before, but …" These long held secrets were sometimes incidents in a person's life where I was able to respond with words like, "Wow! God was really looking after you then, wasn't He?" Or, "God really blessed you in that situation." With eyes of faith, I was able to see *how* God had been with a person at critical times in their life. I often received the reply, "Yes, He was, wasn't He?" Or, "Yes, He did." These were words spoken with surprise and pleasant realisation that they were not alone in the world, but that the God who gave them life was actively looking after them and being intimately involved in their life, even if they hadn't realised it at the time. It is clear, when we listen to people's stories with the eye of faith, we can see the hand of God directing, protecting and leading them. Helping a person see how God is with them is a step towards them coming to know the peace of God which Christ has brought to the world by his own suffering.

A significant story in the Bible is the incident when Jesus and his disciples were in a boat and a powerful storm threatened to overwhelm them (Mark 4:35 – 41). The details of this incident are worth a close look. Jesus had spent the whole day teaching the crowds (Mark 4:1). He taught them many things about the kingdom of God, some of which they struggled to understand. He had to explain things later on to his disciples, away from the crowds (vv.10 – 11). It seems that even after this private lesson, the disciples also still lacked understanding (v.40). It is an exhausting experience to put a lot of effort into teaching to have your students at the end of the day not understand what you have been talking about. It was a long day for Jesus and at the end of it he was keen to get away from the crowds (v.35). He and his disciples got into a boat to cross the lake. On the way Jesus fell asleep. It had been an exhausting day.

While they were crossing the lake a great windstorm blew up and threatened their safety. Waves began breaking into the boat and it was filling with water. They thought they were about to die (vv.37 – 38). Now, remember that some of these men were experienced fishermen. Before they began to follow Jesus they had made their living by fishing on this very lake. They were skilful boating men with experience in these waters, yet, in this storm they feared for their lives. This indicates the severity of the storm. It was like none other in their experience. It was more severe than these capable men thought they were able to handle.

Talk about a crisis. Being in fear of our life is probably the worst crisis we could be in. Imagine what the non-fishermen among this group were feeling at the time. "If these experienced fishermen can't handle this, we are doomed!" And where was Jesus? In the back of the boat, asleep! Asleep? How could he sleep through this?

Now, imagine that at least some of these disciples had begun to ask the question, "Why?" "Why did we leave the safe shoreline tonight of all nights? Why has God allowed this to happen to us?" But, remember, that is the wrong question to be asking. Rather than ask, "why", they should have been asking the question, "How? How is God in this storm, in this boat, with us?" I think you've probably guessed the answer to that question. There is God, in the back of the boat with them in the midst of this raging storm, and he is asleep. Of course, at this stage the disciples had not yet understood that Jesus is God, and this is what he rebukes as their lack of faith in v.40. But there he is. God with them, in the back of the boat.

While the storm was raging and the disciples were in fear of their lives, Jesus was asleep. With our eye of faith, we can see that in this crisis, God was not some far away deity who was not aware and did not care what happened to people in this world. God was right there with them in the midst of this crisis. He was not standing to the side and watching on, perhaps ready to jump in at the last minute if things got worse. God was there in the boat with them. He was going through the same experience they were going through. Yet his response to the storm was one very different to the response of the disciples. Jesus was asleep! The storm was raging, the disciples were afraid for their lives, and Jesus was calm. So calm, he slept.

In this scene there are two very different responses to what seems to be a crisis situation. One is fear, the other is calm. If you have ever asked the question of how God might be with you in a particularly difficult situation you can be assured of two things. The first is that God is with you. He is not at some uncaring distance. He is not standing by at a short distance to pull you out at the last minute. God is there with you (Matthew 28:20) experiencing the same ups and downs of the wild storm at sea that you are experiencing. God is there with you, experiencing life with you. Feeling the same things you're feeling. The second thing you can be sure of is that God is not worried about it. God's got this. He has it all under control. As you're hanging onto the boat for dear life, you might be screaming into the howling wind, "How is this in control?" But the Creator is with you. He who created the sea and the wind is right there in the midst of the storm, experiencing the same stomach-in-the-mouth retching, that you are experiencing. And He is so calm about all this that He could well be asleep.

The scene shows us that the God who is with us in life and in our crisis, is in control. After being wakened by the disciples, Jesus simply said, "Peace. Be still," and the wind stopped and there was a great calm (Mark 4:39). Just like that. A gentle breeze. A glassy sea. The Creator had ordered His creation, and it had obeyed. This is the One who is with us. What do we have to be afraid of?

There is an even deeper encouragement to us in the exegesis of Mark 4:35 – 41. At the end of this incident, when the storm has been calmed, Mark tells us that the disciples, "were filled with great fear" (v. 41). The storm, which had caused the disciples to be in fear for their lives (v. 38) had ceased. The wind had stopped and the sea was calm, no longer breaking into the boat. Why would the disciples now be filled with great fear? They ask the question, "Who then is this, that even the wind and the sea obey him?" (v. 41b) It is a reasonable question, but it is probably the answer to this question, which they would have known only too well, that raises their fear beyond that which they had felt at the height of the storm. Psalm 107:28 – 29 says, "Then they cried to the LORD in their trouble, and he delivered them from their distress. He made the storm be still, and the waves of the sea were hushed." (ESV) The disciples are fully aware that it is only YAWEH Who can still the storm and hush the sea. The disciples' level of fear is raised because of their sudden realisation that, in the person of Jesus, they are sitting in the presence of the Creator Himself. But further, Psalm 107 makes it clear that, as YAWEH makes the storm still, it is He who is responsible for creating the storm in the first place (Psalm 107:23 – 27).

Here is the deeper encouragement to us. Not only does Mark 4:35 – 41 encourage us to know that God is with us in our greatest distress, but He also created the situation that has led to our distress (Psalm 107:25). This thought may not bring comfort to a person in distress. It may, in fact, cause more distress. I have a friend who, when her two-year-old daughter died, was so angry with God, she gave up any trust in him altogether. Such a reaction is quite understandable. We question the goodness of God if He is responsible for bringing pain and suffering on us. But, if it is not God who raises the storms of life, we are in great trouble. It means that God is not in control of His creation. This is not to say that God is responsible for evil in the world. The book of Job makes it clear how Satan must ask permission and God sets the boundaries within which he can work (Job 1:6 – 12, 2:1 – 6). It is Satan who brings evil upon us, but the Bible is clear that God is still in control.

The fact that God is in control, is a great encouragement to us. It means that whatever situation we are in, whether it be enjoying the good things of life or facing disaster and tragic loss, we can know two things. The first is that a disaster does not mean that God has lost control. The disaster may cause us the worst possible imaginable pain, but God is still in control. In fact, if God is not in control, we should be in greater fear. If God can't handle and deal with what is going on in His creation, we have no hope of any good or positive outcome. The second thing is that God is right there with us, experiencing the same pain and loss, caused by the disaster, as we are feeling but, He is calm and in control. Our loss may still be palpable, but it is tempered by the knowledge that God is in control, from beginning to end, and that in all of this, He is working His purposes out. If I can understand that the disaster which I'm going through is somehow achieving the purposes of God to His glory, I am encouraged to know that I am still within God's plan, and I also know that He has not left me, but is still with me, even in the pain and loss I experience.

The aim of pastoral care is to be to the person we're caring for as God would be to them. We may not be able to calm the raging storm, but we are able to just be there for the person we are caring for. As Jesus was with his disciples in the boat, in the storm, the pastor can be with people in life and in crisis and be calm, because we know God's got this. We know God is in control from beginning to end.

God seeks to be in relationship with us. This relationship restores us to the life we were meant to have. Pastoral care says to a person, "Here is life! You are not alone. You have a person who cares for you and will be with you in life and through this crisis." In saying this, the pastor is demonstrating the character of God. In the garden of Eden God said, "Here is life! Eat any fruit you like, except that one. Don't eat the fruit of the tree of the knowledge of good and evil. If you eat that fruit, you will surely die" (Genesis 2:16 – 17). And yet humanity mucked it up, plunging ourselves into crisis. And then, even in the crisis of our own making, God comes to us and says, "Here is life! And that life is in My Son." (1 John 5:11. John 10:10).

A pastor was ministering in an affluent part of the city. A member of his church, Henry, told him that his 16-year-old son had slept with the girl next door and she was now pregnant. So embarrassed was the son that he had stolen money from the family and had now run away. Henry was very angry. He wanted to find his son and beat him. In this chapter we are considering expressing the character of God in pastoral care. Note that Henry's response here to his son's behaviour would probably not express God's character. Henry is right to be angry. It is an appropriate and natural response to such a situation. God is angry with sin. But Henry's desire to beat his son does not express the character of God. God did, on occasion, physically punish Israel for their disobedience and we can all quote the verse, "Spare the rod and spoil the child" (see Proverbs 13:24 and other verses in Proverbs about discipline). But consider how

God treats us today in our own disobedience. He does not beat us. It is quite wrong to tell a person they have become sick, for example, because God is punishing them for some disobedience. I say this fully aware of Paul's words to the Corinthians that, "many of you are weak and ill, and some have died" (1 Corinthians 11:30) because they ate and drank, "without discerning the body" (1 Corinthians 11:29). Unless you are an apostle writing Scripture, or have a direct word from God, avoid such pronouncements. Part of our pastoral response to Henry will be to encourage him to express God's character towards his son.

Henry's wife was very upset and afraid. The younger children in the family were confused and scared. So many issues faced this pastor, he was perplexed about how he might be alongside Henry and his family as God would be. Where should he begin? How could he bring pastoral care to Henry, to his wife, to the other children and to the son who had run away? What practical steps could he take to help this family in crisis? How could he express the character of God in pastoral care?

The pastor was greatly disturbed about another issue. Henry's son had been a prominent member of the church youth group. He had expressed his own faith in Jesus and was regular at the youth Bible study group on Friday nights. Naturally the pastor had concerns for what had happened to this young man. As Henry was sharing his own distress at his son's behaviour the pastor's attention turned away from Henry. When the pastor heard about the son his attention turned to the son. He began to worry how a young Christian man could engage in teenage sex, steal from his family and run away. The pastor's thoughts turned to how he might find Henry's son. He wondered who in the youth group might know anything. He began to think about what he would say to Henry's son. The pastor began to ask Henry questions about his son, more concerned now about the son than what effect this had all had on Henry, the person in front of him. By shifting his attention, the pastor was no longer listening to Henry. This shift gave Henry the impression that the pastor didn't really care about what was going on for Henry himself.

There is an important lesson here for pastoral care. To be an effective pastoral counsellor, focus must stay with the person being cared for. Just as starting to tell our own stories shifts the focus, so does concentrating on an aspect of the person's story that is not their focus. Henry had come to his pastor because he was concerned how to care for his family in this current situation. Henry was distressed and sought pastoral care. While he had an obvious concern for his son who had run away, his immediate concern was how to care for his whole family, how to support his upset wife, how to care for his confused younger children. In fact, with all this stress Henry just wanted some comfort for himself. This was not a selfish desire. Henry knew what he had to do for his family. He had already started some of the process to care for them. But as he had this shock and the stress the situation had put on his family, Henry just wanted to know that someone cared for him. He simply wanted to share his burden. Unfortunately, because his pastor had been distracted by the son's sinful behaviour, Henry did not receive the pastoral care he had come to his pastor for. The lesson for the pastor is to stay focussed on the person in front of you. This is the person who is struggling to understand how God is with them in this crisis.

Henry's situation is the norm in pastoral care. There is never just one issue to deal with. There are multiple issues with multiple layers. The pastoral care task is to sort out which issue is the most pressing for the person seeking help. It is not about which issue I, as the pastoral counsellor, think is the most important. Real pastoral care will ask Henry. We may offer all sorts of practical help. But what does Henry want? What does Henry see as his immediate need? Why has he come to his pastor for care? It may be that Henry has come to his pastor simply for emotional support, as was in fact the case. He may be feeling he has let the family down. He may be feeling that he is a bad father. We will never know until we ask. We must check in with Henry about what he feels his immediate need is.

When Jesus encountered the woman at the well (John 4), he did not assume what she needed. For example, he did not offer to draw water from the well, saving her that hard physical task. Jesus did not assume this was what the woman needed. Of course, Jesus didn't need to ask her what her real, most pressing need was. Jesus had insight into this woman's real need. Unlike Jesus, we do not have such divine insight. Instead, we need to ask. Even if we think their greatest need is as obvious as the nose on their face, we still ask. Jesus focused on the woman's most pressing need because he had divine insight. For us to express the character of God in pastoral care, we do not need divine insight. We need to look for the most pressing need simply by asking. Expressing God's character in pastoral care is to minister to the most pressing need of the person we are caring for.

To understand Henry's immediate need, we ask him, but we don't start asking a bunch of questions. "Do you need money? Do you need food? Can I drive you somewhere to look for your son?" Being bombarded by questions like this does not communicate care. It communicates that I'm looking for a solution to a problem. If I'm talking with Henry, I'm not facing a problem. I'm facing Henry. Pastoral care is not about finding solutions to problems. Pastoral care is about supporting a person through their process of dealing with life. The question for the pastoral carer becomes, "How do I support Henry?" To understand this, I will listen carefully to what Henry says. I will follow the process of how Henry is reacting to his situation and seek to support him in this process. When I have listened, and have some understanding of Henry's need, I will then check in with him. I will ask something like, "It sounds like you are deeply hurt by your son's behaviour. Is that right?"

We will discuss the nature and importance of *process* and of listening, more fully in Chapter Six. There, we will also discuss what is good listening and how we can do it well. But before we get there, here is a small introduction to the idea of process.

I have said before that pastoral care is not about solving problems. Pastoral care is about supporting people, whether they are in crisis or not. That support will express God's character. We will seek to support a person the way that God would support them. Pastoral care touches the whole-of-life. *Process* is observing how a person is dealing with a situation and seeking to help them through that process. Sometimes a person finds that so many things have gone wrong, they really don't know where to begin. They may be in shock and literally don't know what to do. Sometimes, in these situations it may be appropriate for the pastoral carer to give some direction, to actually tell the person what they should do. But these are rare occasions. Normally a crisis situation will bring confusion for the person experiencing it. The pastoral task is to help them through that confusion, to understand their own process. The pastoral task is not to offer solutions to a problem. It is to help a person to be clear in their own mind of what is happening to them emotionally. This is what I mean when I speak about *process*. Process looks at how a person is dealing with their situation and helps them think through that process so that they feel empowered to deal with their own situation.

When a person understands the important thing in a crisis is to deal with process, how the situation is affecting them, they will begin to understand how God is in the situation with them. They will begin to see how, even in the midst of crisis, they are not alone but in fellowship with God. They will begin to understand how their crisis is far less important than their fellowship with God. As pastors help a person through this process, they are expressing the character of God in pastoral care by drawing alongside and by being with the person.

Our fellowship with God is not only an individual fellowship. For evangelicals, with our emphasis on the need for an individual to make a personal decision to follow Christ, we tend to think of fellowship with God as something personal and not corporate. We forget that our fellowship is with God and with each other. When we finally get to heaven, we will be having fellowship not only with God but with a whole lot of others as well. When we gather with God's people on Sundays in our local church we are gathering in fellowship with other believers. Therefore, in the next chapter we consider the importance of our Sunday gatherings.

5

GETTING SUNDAY RIGHT

WHAT ARE WE SUPPOSED TO BE DOING ON SUNDAY? – A THEOLOGY OF CHURCH

Throughout this book when I have used the word "church" I have been thinking of the local congregation. I do not mean "Denomination", nor do I mean the sum total of all Christians throughout the world. Church means gathering. Church is a gathering of people in the same place at the same time. Generally, when the New Testament uses the word church, it has on view this local gathering. Paul writes to the church in Corinth for example. But he writes to the churches in Galatia and the saints in Ephesus and Philippi. He writes to the saints and faithful brothers in Christ at Colossae but to the "church of the Thessalonians". To the Romans Paul has written, "to all those who are in Rome, loved by God, called to be holy".

By reading these different terms of address I hope you can see Paul's understanding of church. In those places where there is a city with a gathering of God's people, Paul calls that gathering church. In the area of

Galatia, he uses the plural because there is more than one gathering. In other places Paul calls God's people saints, the holy ones. The local gathering of God's people is the holy church of God. The local gathering is not a part of the church. It is the church. It is a gathering of saints. This gathering of the saints is a full expression of the gathering in heaven around the throne of God. The writer to the Hebrews says, "you have come to Mount Zion and to the city of the living God, the heavenly Jerusalem, and to innumerable angels in festal gathering, and to the assembly of the firstborn who are enrolled in heaven, and to God, the judge of all, and to the spirits of the righteous made perfect, and to Jesus, the mediator of a new covenant, and to the sprinkled blood that speaks a better word than the blood of Abel." (Hebrews 12:22 – 24. ESV)

THE CORE OF PASTORAL CARE

God's people delight to meet with God's people. We delight to hear God's word. We delight to be in the presence of the Word of Life Himself as He promised He would be whenever two or more of us get together (Matthew 18:20 & 28:20). By our prayers we look forward to the opportunity of participating with God in what He is doing in the world. After all, this is what heaven is like. Church, our Sunday gathering, is heaven on earth. Our earthly meetings give a visible expression on earth of the heavenly gathering. No wonder it's a delight to gather with other members of the body of Christ. No wonder the saints are asking their pastors to, *please, get Sunday right.*

In the introduction I suggested that members of God's church are asking their pastors to "get Sunday right". I think this is the core of pastoral care. While pastoral care is the core of what pastor teachers do, what pastor teachers do on Sundays is the core of their pastoral care of the saints. In this chapter my focus is on how the Sunday gathering is an opportunity for the pastor teacher to equip the saints for the work of ministry, for building the body. But this is a secondary focus of our Sunday gatherings. In church, in our local Sunday meeting, our focus is God. We gather to give a visible expression on earth to the heavenly gathering. God is among us, and we acknowledge His presence by singing His praises, by prayer and by listening to His word.

In church on Sundays our focus is God. In this sense, church is not for the people, but for God. We gather to praise and petition God. But church is also for the people. The task of the pastor teacher is to so shape the Sunday meeting that God's people are focused on God. Meeting together in our local church will also teach us to take this focus on God into our week. This is pastoral care.

It is in the Sunday meeting of God's people that the pastor teacher has the opportunity to care for God's people, to exercise the *cure of souls*, to equip the saints for the work of ministry, both in the church and in the world. The pastor will think through every part of the service theologically so that it is one big exercise in pastoral care. Of course, *getting Sunday right* is not limited to what we do on Sundays in our main meetings. *Getting Sunday right* involves creating a community of God's people where those who follow Jesus belong and learn in that community how to be whole-of-life Christians. By "whole-of-life Christians" I mean, not dividing the sacred from the secular. Not succumbing to a modernist divide that insisted religion was a private matter where a person's faith is separated from everything else they do in the world. Whole-of-life Christians will live as Christian people in their homes, in their workplaces, neighbourhoods and communities. *Getting Sunday right* will equip them to do this.

Getting Sunday right involves equipping the saints to build the body of Christ and to live Christianly in the world. The body of Christ is the community the faithful belong to. As such, getting Sunday right is at the core of pastoral care. The saints not only want to come to church and honour God and feel uplifted. They also want to go into the world prepared to think Christianly about their daily activities. They want to develop a sense of confidence that this Christian life is worth living. They want to know that being Christian in the world is the best thing they can do. In a world that makes comedy movies about a 40-year-old virgin and laughs at Christian morality, the single Christian wants support and encouragement to know that a life of chastity is a life worth living. And, as a 40-year-old virgin, they want to be equipped to have a positive Christian influence in the world. They want to be equipped as part of a Christian community which supports them to live as Jesus lived and directs His people to go on living. They want to be able to speak to a secular society about the appropriateness of Christian chastity and to be respected for that lifestyle.

Getting Sunday right is real pastoral care because it equips God's people to live in the world. It helps husbands and wives to truly reflect the relationship between Christ and his church in their own marriages (Ephesians 5:25-33). It helps fathers not to exasperate their children but to bring them up in the love and discipline of the Lord (Ephesians 6:4). It helps bosses and workers to relate well to each other (Ephesians 6:5 – 9). It helps us all to be strong in the Lord (Ephesians 6:10). It helps men, women and children to engage with the world in a godly manner so that they bring a Christian influence into the world rather than take on the world's values. Getting Sunday right helps the Christian doctor to be a *Christian* doctor, a *Christian* builder to be a Christian builder, a

Christian truck driver to be a *Christian* truck driver.

This chapter is not about what shape a Sunday service should take in terms of whether it should have Gregorian chants or modern rock bands. There are too many Christian traditions for me to suggest that any one way of "doing Sunday" should be the one everyone must follow. The richness of our different traditions reflects the freedom God has given us in life. We are able to shape our meetings in ways that are culturally appropriate, historically faithful to our tradition, theologically expressive of our beliefs, or simply according to personal preference. None is right and others wrong. What the pastor teacher will consider in preparing for Sunday church, is what the shape of our meetings says about and to God. The pastor will give attention to how the Sunday meetings encourage the saints for the building of the body of Christ. The goal of this encouragement is so that we attain unity, maturity, and the measure of the stature of the fullness of Christ.

In their book, *Emerging Churches - creating Christian community in postmodern cultures*, Eddie Gibbs and Ryan Bolger (SPCK, 2006), after a comprehensive study of more than fifty Christian leaders, identify nine practices of Christian churches, three of which they believe are core to the life of a vibrant church. These are firstly, identifying with the life and teaching of Jesus. Secondly, recognising a whole of life Christian commitment where there is no divide between the sacred and the secular. And, thirdly, identifying as a Christian community or family. These practices are no radical new teaching. They are practices which are core to Christian living that Gibbs and Bolger identified in what they describe as effective Christian churches. These are the core practices of a Christian church the pastor teacher will work on to get Sunday right. Pastor teachers will be working on creating a community of God's people. They will not just focus on care for individuals who attend a Sunday meeting. They will be encouraging those individuals to form community in Christ.

The apostle Paul envisages the community of God's people as a body. It is no ordinary body. When Paul speaks of the body, he is not just using an analogy. He is speaking about the body of Christ. While in 1 Corinthians 12:12 it may appear as though Paul is using an analogy, he makes it clear that he is not simply using a humorous illustration. In verse 27 Paul says, "you are the body of Christ". This is a serious, sacred matter. You, the church of God, are the body of Christ. This community we belong to is Christ's own and each believer is a member. No wonder the saints want pastors to get Sunday right. They want to rightly express the body of Christ in this world.

Getting Sunday right is a recognition that the Sunday church services are the major event of the Christian week, and these gatherings must express the character of God, equip the saints for ministry and build the body of Christ. Our Sunday gatherings give expression to the fact that we are the body of Christ. Pastoral care helps us to work out what part of the body each of us is so that we build the body together in love.

WHAT IS ESSENTIAL TO SUNDAY

Clearly, there are things that go into a Sunday service that define them as Christian. I once attended a church service, led by a layperson, which had no prayer. We had plenty of singing, and maybe you could say we prayed as we sang some of those songs. We had some Bible reading. We had a statement of faith, and we had a sermon. But we had no prayer. It was a strange experience. The people of God had come together. Surely the major reason we do that is to praise God for what he has done for us in our Lord Jesus Christ. There was some praise in our singing. But that was all. There were no intercessions. No opportunity to bring before our great God our desires in petition. No opportunity to pray for a broken and divided world. No opportunity to uphold to our God the poor and needy in our society. No opportunity to pray for the sick or the spread of the gospel. No opportunity to pray for ourselves to live godly lives.

Prayer really is an essential element in a Christian gathering as the church of God. Prayer is the privilege God gives us to join Him in the work He is doing in the world. When God wants to do something, He firstly stirs up His people to pray and thereby join Him in that work. What a privilege prayer is. When we don't pray, we are really saying we don't believe that God wants to do anything in the world at this time. Or, maybe, we just don't see the world the way God sees it and we are not stirred with compassion for the lost, the sick, the dying, for world governments, or the spiritual growth of God's own people.

I have pointed out that this service which had no prayer was led by a layperson. This does not mean I think Sunday services must be led by ordained people. It was simply a fact that this particular service was led by a layperson. I point it out because I think, ultimately, the responsibility for the Sunday meeting is that of the ordained clergy. Clergy don't have to lead the service. It is a good thing that lay people lead the service. It is a good thing that lay people are involved and are not simply observers. But it is the responsibility of the person appointed by the congregation or the denomination, the person who has the title of *pastor*, to ensure that we get Sunday right. This is pastoral care. If the person with the responsibility of pastoral care of the congregation is not going to lead the Sunday meeting, it remains their responsibility to ensure that those who are leading are well trained to do so and that the things they will include (and exclude) are appropriate.

The New Testament tells us about elements of what the first Christians included in their meetings. These are mainly descriptive and are not necessarily something to follow. An example is what Luke tells us in Acts 2:42 about the first meetings after Pentecost. The new believers devoted themselves to the apostles' teaching and the fellowship, to the breaking of bread and the prayers. These seem like excellent things to be doing together with God's people. Doing these things in our Sunday meetings will go a long way towards getting Sunday right.

The New Testament also gives us some directives on what we should be doing when we come together. Paul's list in 1 Corinthians 14:26 is not exhaustive nor is it directive but he does give instruction following this. At the end of the list, Paul's instruction is that all things should be done for building up. He goes on in vv. 27 – 35 to explain that this *building up* is done through order and submission. In these verses there are three different groups in the congregation the apostle instructs must not speak at certain times. This instruction is for the good order of the assembly, which is for the building up of God's people.

In Ephesians 4:12, as we have already seen, the purpose of Christ's gift is so that the saints are equipped for building the body of Christ. It is clear from this passage and from 1 Corinthians 14 the apostle is concerned that Christian meetings should be about building Christ's body. We need to carefully understand that building Christ's body is not about building up God's people as individuals. Building up individuals sounds like I should go to church so that I can be built up. It sounds like I should go to church so that I can become a stronger Christian. But this is not the focus of Ephesians 4. The focus in Ephesians 4 is that the act of building will equip God's people collectively to be mature in Christ. It is about building a community, or rather, a body. The community we are building is the body of Christ. As we build this community we are aiming for maturity. This maturity leads to godly living both in the church and in the public sphere. As we read on in Ephesians 4 Paul's focus is on godly, theologically correct, God honouring behaviour in church and in the marketplace.

As we shape what we do together in our Sunday meetings these are the things we will consider. Our primary consideration will be towards how we can so shape these activities that the whole congregation is pastorally cared for, to God's glory. We will think through how what we do this Sunday will equip the saints for ministry. How what we do in church will equip God's people to speak the truth in love (vv. 15 & 25), how not to live as the Gentiles do (v. 17), how to put off our old self (v. 22), to be renewed in the spirit of our minds (v. 23), and to put on the new self (v. 24). The importance of a day's work is also an aspect of Christian maturity (v. 28). We will think through how our Sunday meetings will encourage God's people to use words that build people up and give grace (v. 29). We will encourage God's people to not grieve the Holy Spirit (v. 30) and to put away all bitterness, wrath and anger, clamour and slander, along with all malice (v. 31). The apostle's final instruction in this passage is to remember that we have been forgiven by God. We should therefore be kind to one another, tender-hearted, and forgiving of one another (v. 32).

Obviously, we will not try to cram all these things into every Sunday gathering. Pastor teachers will keep these imperatives in Ephesians 4 in the back of mind as they prepare the Sunday meeting. They will be thinking about which aspects of Christian living the saints need more encouragement in. They will be aware of a tendency to ride their own hobby horses and ensure their care of the saints is balanced. They will seek to ensure that the whole sweep of Ephesians 4:15 – 32 is covered on a regular basis in the church's teaching cycle.

Encouraging God's people in the behaviours listed in Ephesians 4 is pastoral care. You will notice that some of these behaviours focus on our relationships with our fellow believers. Others relate to how the Christian person will behave in the world. Equipping God's people for ministry to each other and to the world is what pastoral care is all about. *Getting Sunday right* is ensuring that the things we do in church encourage the saints to minister to each other and to be an example of godly living in the public sphere.

When we think about the Christian behaviour that so irritated the Emperor Julian (see Chapter Three), we must ask the question about what so changed in the lives of those Christians that they saw the importance of caring for the vulnerable and marginalised. Also, perhaps more importantly, how did they have the courage to go against accepted social norms to bring that care to the vulnerable and marginalised?

It would be true to say that the answer to the first part of that question is that the Christians of that time had come to understand the grace of God in their own lives. They had understood that in their time of need God had come to them and rescued them. They further understood that this grace of God to them also empowered them to reach out to others suffering the burdens of this life. Helping God's people, therefore, to deeply understand the grace of God in our lives and how this understanding will affect our behaviour in our daily living is a part of what the pastor teacher will teach the saints. Teaching about God's grace, and a constant reminder of God's grace, for a people whose natural tendency is to gravitate towards law keeping, is the pastoral care which will help us to get Sundays right.

It would also be true in answer to the second part of the question to say the Christian people of Emperor Julian's time had recognised, that in reaching out to them, Christ had done so in the face of extreme opposition. Suffering the ire of opponents is not an excuse to avoid bringing the love and grace of God to a broken and hurting world. These Christians were well equipped to live as Christians in the world. Someone was getting Sunday right way back in the fourth century. Someone was pastorally caring for these Christians.

BEING CHRISTIAN IN THE WORLD

Some years ago, when I was ministering as a hospital chaplain a new group of graduate doctors arrived in the hospital. A few months later I discovered that a large number of the dozen or so new doctors were Christians. I was surprised to discover this at the time because there was nothing in their behaviour, in either dealing with the patients or with other staff, to suggest they were Christians. Their behaviour and their attitudes seemed to be the same as all the others. Now, I'm not suggesting that Christians need to go around with signs on their heads, but I do think there are certain behaviours and attitudes that will distinguish Christian people. I have seen many a new graduate doctor, proud of their superior knowledge and status, being more concerned about their reputation than care for their patients. These Christian doctors didn't stand out from this sort of attitude.

I also discovered that, while at Med School, all of these Christian doctors had attended weekly campus Bible studies. They had been well taught and had a deep knowledge of the Bible. But, somehow, this deep knowledge had not equipped these people to think through what it meant to be a *Christian* doctor. The great Bible teaching they had received had not, therefore, pastorally cared for them. It had not equipped them for the work of ministry. Clearly, they also had not received this care in their home churches. Nobody had the pastoral care of these young people in mind, and they had therefore not been prepared to live in the world as Christian people. It is all well and good to faithfully teach the word of God and to give Christian people a deep knowledge of the Scriptures, but it has to help them be Christian in the world. If Bible teaching doesn't do this, it doesn't have a pastoral focus. Teaching the Bible just to fill Christian heads with Bible knowledge helps only to separate the sacred from the secular. It does nothing to help the sacred people of God to live in the secular world.

We have to question, if Bible teaching doesn't have a pastoral focus, then why are we teaching at all? Do we simply want people to have head knowledge? Surely, we want people to know God and to be equipped to live for God in the world. Abraham Kuruvilla has made the point that preaching must be more than propositional. It must be transformational.[24] The pastor teacher must not only do the exegesis. They must also work out the hermeneutic for God's people in the 21st century. Whatever shape our Sunday meetings take, we must think through how they will equip the saints. This is *getting Sunday right*. This is pastoral care. This is the *cure of souls*.

---

24   Abraham Kuruvilla. *A Vision for Preaching – Understanding the Heart of Pastoral Ministry*. Baker Academic. Grand Rapids. 2015.

DEALING WITH DIVISIONS

We have noted above some of the things the New Testament directs us to do when we meet together. There is also clear teaching on what not to do. In 1 Corinthians 11:17 – 22 the apostle Paul records some appropriate yet very harsh words. He indicates that when the people of God in Corinth came together it was not for the better but for the worse.

Some of you will have had the experience of coming away from church feeling the worse for it. This is often because of divisions in the church. One group wants this, and another group wants that. Nobody is satisfied and all leave feeling very uneasy. This is the situation Paul addresses in these verses. He points out that their coming together is for the worse because there are divisions among them (v. 18). In particular the apostle is concerned about the way the Corinthians have been treating the Lord's supper. One person goes hungry. Another person gets drunk (v. 21). People in the church of God are humiliated (v. 22). This is no way for the people of God to behave when they come together, and Paul roundly condemns such behaviour. Humiliating those who have nothing is no way to build the body of Christ.

When we come together as the church of God, we recognise our unity in Christ and treat each other as Christ has treated us. This is how we get Sunday right. Our primary focus is on God. We come together to declare His praise. Our secondary focus will be a vision of pastoral care. We will seek to be giving our souls wings so that we will rise up and praise our God in the gathering of His people.

The way we "do church" will teach God's people how to be Christian. For example, *how* we pray as the church of God will teach us how to pray on our own and in our families. *What* we pray for in church will teach us what to pray for on our own and in our families. The priorities the pastor teacher sets in the service will teach the congregation what priorities each member should be setting for themselves in their daily living. This is the point at which the pastor teacher needs to think very carefully about how the Sunday service equips the saints for ministry. If there is a disconnect between the priorities the pastor teacher sets on Sundays and the priorities members of the congregation face in their average daily lives, we will not be getting Sunday right.

To get Sunday right, the priorities that shape our Sunday meetings will have an affinity with the priorities members face during the week. When faced with ordinary, everyday life issues, a Christian person who has been well pastorally cared for on Sunday will be confident that they can have a positive Christian interaction with that issue during the week. They will know what a Christian response is and have an assurance they are able to confidently engage with it.

THE BEAUTY OF SUNDAYS

In saying that our Sunday meetings will have an affinity with our week, I am not suggesting that our activities in church should look like what we do during the week. The very reason Christians meet on Sundays is to celebrate the resurrection. The resurrection changes everything. Jesus rose on a Sunday morning. Very early on, the Christians, realising they were no longer bound by the Law to keep the Sabbath because they now kept it in Christ who has fulfilled the Law, began to meet on Sundays to celebrate the resurrection.

Celebrating the resurrection takes us out of the mundane. It says to the ordinariness of life that in Christ there is new life. It is life like you have never known before. It is life in reconciliation with God. It is life abundant. This celebration takes us away from the world and directs our attention to something magnificent. Meeting with God's people on a Sunday morning to celebrate God's triumph over death makes life worth living.

A friend of mine told me that as a boy, life was so terrible growing up in a poor, abusive, and alcoholic home that he found going to church gave him life. He said it was magnificent to be in the midst of God's people, singing praises to God and celebrating their life in Him. It gave him a different life experience. It lifted him and gave his soul wings. It was magnificent. It was joyful. It was caring and powerful. It held him as the person he is, created in the image of God. It lifted him out of his daily abuse, and he realised it was not his fault. He was not to blame for the lack of money. He was not to blame for his father seeking solace in alcohol. He was not responsible for his father's anger and abuse. He was a child of God. Valued by God to the extent Jesus came to serve him, not abuse him.

My friend found in his boyhood that his pastor *got Sunday right*. By simply providing a place of meaningful, encouraging and uplifting Christian fellowship celebrating what God has done for us in Christ, my friend was empowered to face his horrible week.

Whatever we do on Sundays, church must remain church. We are the bride of Christ. That relationship of submission, obedience and love must find expression in our gatherings. It is wonderful to come away from church feeling that as we have met with God's people, we have met with God who was in our midst. If our Sunday gatherings are to pastorally care for God's people, they must at least do this. They must so uplift us that we feel empowered to face whatever the coming week might throw at us.

There is nothing better than the proverbial *hymn sandwich* week after week to make going to church feel like a chore. The hymn sandwich is a service that has had no thought put into its preparation. The service is thoughtlessly interspersed with some prayers, a Bible reading and a sermon with a few hymns thrown in. Pastor teachers should avoid hymn sandwiches at all costs. They become a boring diet very quickly if served up weekly. *Getting Sunday right* is at least uplifting the church so they can face the coming week.

A church gathering that helped him face the coming week was certainly a positive thing in my friend's boyhood. But imagine if it had done more. Image if my friend had been equipped to face his father's violence with a positive Christian response. Imagine 50, 100, 200 people in the Lord's church equipped to face their week, not just running on the reserves they filled up with on Sunday, but equipped to speak into their week with a positive Christian voice. Imagine a doctor who is not deceived by the trappings of worldly status and wealth but is inspired to serve her patients. A builder who desires to serve her clients by providing quality workmanship because this is what Jesus would have done. Image Christian citizens engaging in the political debate with a Christian mind, demonstrating an irenic spirit as opposed to the attacks on character so prevalent in modern political debate.

Equipping the saints to engage in the world with these types of Christian behaviour and responses, is *getting Sunday right*. This is pastoral care. The pastor teacher needs to plan the Sunday gatherings. Thought needs to be put into the planning, understanding the issues congregation members are grappling with during their average week. These may be individual issues the pastor knows about because he or she has been engaging with their congregation and understands what is happening in their lives. By addressing individual issues, I do not mean the pastor will address anyone's personal issues from the pulpit. But you can find a way to proclaim the Bible's teaching about issues members of the church will face personally in their lives.

Issues the saints are grappling with will include widespread community issues which Christians are wanting to understand from a biblical perspective. They do not just want to understand what the Bible says on the issue. They don't just want to be filled with good biblical knowledge. They want to know how to use that knowledge in the world. The people of God want to work out how they can be Christian and have a Christian voice to engage graciously with the secular world on current issues. This is what they are asking for when they ask their pastors to *get Sunday right*.

Our Sunday gatherings will have a three-way focus. Our first focus is God. We are meeting on what we call, "The Lord's Day". Most societies and cultures celebrate special days. They may be the nation's Foundation Day, the Sovereign's birthday, a particular day to commemorate a victory in war. Each of these days is celebrated with great ceremony and many special events, concerts and formalities. These types of celebrations are only once a year. The celebration of our Lord's Day is every week. His day has far more significance and consequence than those national celebrations. We should give it the significance it deserves.

When we gather on the Lord's Day in our local church we want to praise and glorify our God. He has won the victory and we are included in the victory parade. Christ has brought us captive (Ephesians 4:8 and Psalm 68:18) and the angels of heaven, and all those who have gone before us (Hebrews 12:1), are singing His praise, cheering us on, and in response, we join the angelic host singing the praise of the Lamb who died but is alive (Revelation 5:12). Christ has been raised from the dead. Death is dead. Sin has lost its sting. We want to shout out to the universe, how great is our God.

Music and song are important ingredients in our Sunday meetings because they reflect heaven and the angels' response to what God has done for us in Christ. Can you imagine what it was like on the first Christmas night in the Bethlehem hinterland when the angel of the Lord was joined by a multitude of the heavenly host praising God? (See Luke 2:13 – 14) The joyful chorus that night must have been the most magnificent the universe has ever heard. That is why we don't use hymns simply to fill a gap or as a mere transition from one aspect of the service to another. If a song, a hymn or a musical interlude is used as a transition, it will speak meaningful words that draw our thoughts from what we have just done to what we are about to do. Whether we use a rock band or Gregorian chants doesn't matter. What matters is that it is meaningful to the Lord's congregation and that it is done decently and in order (1 Corinthians 14:40). Thought has to be put into it so that it truly honours Christ and that it also pastorally cares for God's people.

A pastor teacher may not be gifted in music. I certainly am not, and I am guilty of throwing together a hymn sandwich because I could not think of what music might be appropriate to the service. In such a case the pastor needs to seek help. Many churches these days have *music pastors*. If a congregation is blessed with someone who can lead the music, the senior pastor needs to coordinate with them about the central theme or focus of this week's service. The senior pastor sets the agenda because this is the person appointed to the *cure of souls*. A congregation dictated to by the organist or choir is a congregation in division.

Senior pastors have the role of pastorally caring for the flock. Together with the ministry of the word of God, they have the role of equipping the saints. Senior pastors are the person responsible for the shape of the Sunday gathering. They are the person responsible for *getting Sunday right*. They may have help in doing this, even lots of help. But the theological shape and the theological reasons are the responsibility of the pastor teacher. The buck stops with the senior pastor. This is how you pastorally care for God's people.

Getting Sunday right is equipping the saints for building the body of Christ. It is feeding the flock to build the body of Christ. It is inspiring the saints with the sacred, so they go joyfully into the secular, confident in the truth of the gospel, confident their godly lifestyle is pleasing to God even in the face of worldly laughter or even hatred. Confident they can speak and act in a godly and graceful manner that respectfully engages with a world view that is contrary to their own world view in Christ.

SUNDAY IS FOR THE SAINTS

As we think about Sunday in these terms, I am suggesting Sunday meetings are for the saints. We shape what we do in our Sunday meetings for the growth of the body of Christ. Primarily, this will focus on speaking to brothers and sisters in Christ. Our Sunday meetings are not evangelistic gatherings. By this, I do not mean we shut our doors to unbelievers. We, as the catholic (universal) church of God welcome all, as does our God. Our meetings will therefore have some sensitivity to the fact that there will be people among us who are searching. They may have been influenced by the interaction they have had with a member of the church in their workplace and have been invited to come along and see and consider Christ. But the focus of the Sunday meeting is the saints and equipping them for building the body of Christ.

While our Sunday meetings are for the saints, by their very nature, our meetings will challenge the unbeliever among us to consider Christ. Paul encourages us to consider what we do in church with a view to how it might affect the outsider (1 Corinthians 14:16 & 23). When we consider carefully what we are doing in church, as Paul in 1 Corinthians 14 is encouraging us to do, the unbeliever will be convicted and will worship God (1 Corinthians 14:24 – 25). But Paul doesn't mean the focus of our meetings should be the outsider or unbeliever. We are to consider the unbeliever in our midst, but our focus is declaring the praises of God, firstly, and striving to excel in building the church, secondly. Our focus, as we praise God, is on equipping the saints.

I used to attend a church that had well thought out liturgy, great music (to my taste), and great preaching. I felt very much a part of this community, being inspired by the Sunday gatherings, and encouraged in midweek small groups. However, our pastor teacher was an evangelist. While he was a great preacher and taught the Bible very well, every sermon came to the point of challenging our beliefs and calling on us to put our trust in Christ. It's great to have the gospel repeated to us, as the wonderful old hymn, "Tell me the old, old story" and Philippians 3:1 remind us. But such a constant application of every text of Scripture shows a laziness on the preacher's part to understand what the Bible says to the saints. It fails in its responsibility to equip the saints for the work of ministry. It fails to build the body of Christ. It also dishes up what becomes a very disappointing bland menu week after week. Such a diet fails in its task of pastoral care.

The sermon should be encouraging the congregation to think how they will live Christ honouring, influential lives during the coming week. If the sermon repeats, week after week, the pastor's favourite themes, the pastor is more than likely not engaging with the text they are preaching on. When God's people want their pastor to get Sunday right, they want to be inspired to go into the world in the following week to have a Christian influence in it. The pastor must be the pastor theologian to help God's people understand how the passage of scripture will help them do this.

CONCLUSION

In this and the previous chapters I have been encouraging senior pastors to think very carefully how to offer pastoral care in the whole of their ministry. Pastoral care should not be thought of as something which is done only for people in crisis. Pastoral care should not be outsourced to psychologists and counsellors. Pastoral care is the work the pastor does. Pastoral care is the work a pastor has been appointed by God to do.

I have given some examples of real situations where I have observed pastors doing a pretty terrible job of pastoral care. I have hinted at how pastors, as under-shepherds, can be more present for the people of God. In the next chapter I give some practical advice on pastoral counselling. I hope it will give you a better idea of what I have been talking about when I have spoken about the importance of process. I hope it will also give you some confidence to sit with a congregation member in crisis and not feel inadequate. The next chapter is not a course in pastoral counselling, but I hope it might whet your appetite enough that you may consider doing such a course with a reputable institution.

6
PASTORAL COUNSELLING

The main aim of this book is to encourage pastor teachers to see their entire ministry in terms of pastoral care. Equipping the saints for the work of ministry is the work of pastoral care, which the pastor teacher does basing the teaching on the Scriptures. I want to reverse the modern trend which sees pastoral care as only something you do for people in crisis. I want to broaden the focus so that pastoral care is seen to be the whole essence of pastoral ministry. Pastoral care has a whole-of-life focus. That does not mean, however, that a pastor teacher does not get involved with people in crisis situations. We live in a fallen world. People suffer. We do things wrongly. We get into trouble. Life is messy. We cannot avoid crisis situations.

This chapter, therefore, is about some basic issues of how to respond to people who find themselves in difficulties. These can be some of the big issues of life or they may be just a situation where a person isn't coping very well with some of the mundane things of life. It can be as seemingly trivial as getting frustrated with being late for an appointment or as big as a relationship breakdown. This chapter is about pastoral counselling. I illustrate with some examples from my own experiences.

PASTORAL CARE ON THE RUN

One issue we must note, is that in pastoral ministry pastoral care often happens on the run. Pastoral care doesn't usually make appointments. Pastoral care mostly does not sit down in a dedicated counselling room and allocate an hour of time to a conversation. On the one hand organised pastoral care takes place in the pulpit, in preparing for the meeting, in designing a program, in the mundane business of running a church. But it is in the most unexpected places people will reveal they are having some difficulties. The pastor teacher will be the pastor on the run. They will stop and listen to the father at morning tea whose son has been taking drugs. They will casually join a conversation where a parishioner is telling anyone who will listen about their irritations with life. They will stop in the supermarket and listen to the frustrated father trying to juggle kids, work and marriage.

I thought about calling these pastoral encounters on the run *micro-pastoral care*, but I don't want the term to diminish the importance of these on the run times of pastoral care. They are important encounters but are also often all that is needed. These quick encounters often change how a person is coping with their situation. On the run pastoral care is important because it often helps to avoid crisis situations. While they may be casual and on the run, such conversations are never small things for the pastor teacher. They can be life changing.

An *on the run* pastoral conversation may be all that is needed for a member of God's church to gain some re-focus. The small things you say may be just enough to encourage the person to know they are not on their own. The few words of pastoral care you offer may be just what the person needs to process what they are going through and develop a new strategy for getting through their situation. Later in this chapter we will see an example of how a few words from her Pastor in an on the run conversation helped Kerry to develop a new strategy for copying with her frustrations.

The pastor should never get in a flap about what to say. People will often not remember what you say but that you took the time. They will remember the love you have shown them. They will remember the fact that you cared enough to stop and listen more so than the words you spoke. Words are important. People will certainly remember uncaring or hurtful words. But if a pastor teacher takes the time to lovingly listen to a person, the person will remember that loving gesture more than they will remember what you said to them.

A pastor teacher should never communicate to members of God's church that they are too busy to spend time. If you are too busy to spend time with the people God has placed under your pastoral care then, what on earth are you doing in ministry? Ministry is about people. A pastor spends time with people. God's people will often say to their pastor, "I know you are busy. I didn't want to disturb you." A pastor will teach the people of God to change this attitude. Pastor teachers will ensure the flock knows their pastor is never too busy to spend time with them.

Recognising that on the run pastoral conversations are important does not mean we don't need to make time to sit down, one to one, in a quiet space to discuss an important issue. For some situations an organised time to discuss an issue is essential. A more meaningful term to describe these dedicated times of pastoral care is *Pastoral Counselling*. In effect pastoral counselling is no different to all of life pastoral care and on the run pastoral care. Each activity involves focused listening with a view to bringing the comfort and encouragement of Christ into people's lives. It is to encourage people to know *how* God is with them in any of life's situations. Using the term *Pastoral Counselling* for those times when we make an appointment to sit with a person for an hour helps us to understand that here we are dealing with a more serious situation of a person in crisis.

In an on the run conversation, we may become aware that a much more focused time and space is needed for meaningful pastoral care to take place. When this is the case, we need to acknowledge this is what is needed. We will need to organise a dedicated time and place. There will be times when other obligations demand our time. We will not be able to give our focussed attention when we have other pressing obligations. At these times we suggest to the person that the issue is an important one and that we should make a time (soon) to discuss it more fully. This will show the person we think the issue is important enough that we will make time for it. Not right now, but within the next day or two. This, in itself, will encourage the person to feel that the pastor has drawn alongside them, and it will usually hold them until you meet.

If an issue arises that will require more time or more privacy than you have at the moment it is not enough to say, "now is not a good time but we must make a time." Good pastoral care of people will put people first. This is not to allow the urgent to replace the important. If we have something else we are committed to at this time, which means we do not have enough time at the moment to deal with a person's need for deeper pastoral care, we will make a time with them to sit and talk. We will show that we are committed to their pastoral care.

As usual, balance is needed. Sometimes there are just some things a member of the congregation needs urgent help with that cannot wait. Sometimes that meeting with the Bishop will have to wait instead, while we give time to a member of Christ's church.

We should also not feel guilty if making a time to see a person later, rather than deal with their issue now, is because the appointment we are committed to now is a personal issue, or simply personal time. If the pastoral issue a member of God's church brings to us is not one of those life and death issues that requires immediate attention, it can wait. The pastor needs to take care of themselves. Simply jumping at every pastoral issue that crosses our path is a recipe for burnout. What use then will you be to those who need your pastoral care?

When I was a hospital chaplain, I received a 3am phone call. This usually meant that someone had died, or was expected to die soon, the family was present and requested a chaplain. On these occasions, I was happy to forgo the sleep and take up the opportunity of bringing God's love to a grieving family. However, this particular call had come from a woman who had earlier that night presented at the Emergency Department. She had been examined and well cared for by the medical staff. They had given her appropriate medication and assured her it was alright for her to go home. At 3am she had decided the best way to get home was to call the chaplain with the expectation that he would drive her home. At 3am the chaplain thought his sleep was a priority. Just as the Emergency medical staff will triage the people who present for treatment, chaplains and pastor teachers need to differentiate the urgent and the important and respond appropriately.

TRIANGULATION

In the 1950s Eric Berne developed an idea he called "Transactional Analysis". He outlined the different roles people play in conflict and how people can change their role in conflict. He said that in conflict, there are three major roles: Parent, Adult, Child. He labelled this description of conflict, "triangulation". Often when we are in conflict with someone we can feel like a child. The other person seems to be like a parent, telling us what to do, disciplining us, and not treating us like the adult we are. Sometimes we can play the role of parent and treat the other person like a child and not an adult. Neither of these roles are healthy between two adults. Clergy particularly need to be careful about playing the role of parent and treating people like the child. If we become aware that we are playing one of these roles we need to stop and become an adult. An adult is a mature person who does not treat other adults like children. An adult is also a mature person who does not take on the role of a child when someone tries to treat them as a parent would treat their children. When we feel like we are being treated like a child, the best thing to do is to respond in a mature adult way and do not allow ourselves to be treated like a child.

Clergy need to be aware that members of the congregation can also seek guidance from their pastor where they treat you more as a parent than another adult. This is not healthy, neither for the church member nor the pastor. I once heard a friend who had a life changing decision to make say, "I can't wait for my pastor to get back from holiday so I can find out what I should do." I'm sure my friend's pastor would have been horrified to hear a member of God's church say this, but it is often the way that members of a church so highly regard the opinion of their pastor, they will take on the role of child. Clergy must be careful not to allow their ego to create unhealthy power relationships.

In 1968 Stephen Karpman developed what he called the "Drama Triangle". He talked about the Oppressor – Victim – Rescuer. In this model the "parent" from Berne's model is the "oppressor". The oppressor tries to control. The person being controlled is the victim. The victim usually doesn't feel they can stand up to the oppressor and therefore looks to a rescuer. Often in pastoral care the person we're talking to will feel they are a victim in their crisis and they will look to the pastoral carer to be their rescuer from the oppressor. We need to be careful that we never become the rescuer in pastoral care. Our goal is to encourage the person we're pastorally caring for to be strong enough to deal with the oppressor themselves. If we play the role of the rescuer, the person will never develop strength to deal with their own situation.

Bill was a pastor teacher who had recently taken a new role as senior minister of a congregation. A few months after his appointment a middle-aged man came to see him. Bill had not met the man before, but Clive told him the previous senior minister had helped him a lot. Clive told Bill how his family was trying to take over the family business and shut him out. Clive admitted to having had some mental health issues, but he was not "mad" and could still make decisions to help the business prosper. Clive came to Bill for help to speak to his family and make them understand that he was still quite capable of running the business. Bill's predecessor had done this for Clive but now he had left, Clive's family were again trying to take control.

Do you see the issues of triangulation in this story? Clive has taken on the role of victim or child, sees his family as oppressor or parent (telling him what to do as though he is a child) and wants Bill to play the role of rescuer. Unfortunately, when Bill's predecessor did what Clive asked, and talked to the family about the situation, he took on the role of rescuer. Clive did not need a rescuer and by Bill's predecessor taking on this role, he has only confirmed that Clive is a child or a victim, not capable of standing up for himself.

Understanding triangulation helps us to understand complicated dynamics in relationships. When we can see who is playing what role, we have a better understanding of the role we might have to play within the dynamic. Usually, that role is not to get involved in the triangulation at all. In pastoral counselling we stay out of the triangulation. Bill's predecessor had joined the triangulation as Clive's rescuer. By doing so, he had not given Clive the pastoral care he needed. Clive was still in the same predicament months later when he came to Bill.

Kerry's husband fell over when he was drunk and had broken his leg. In hospital he fell out of bed and broke his arm. Kerry complained about his poor treatment, but the hospital staff seemed to ignore her complaints. Not knowing how to take her complaint further, and being worried for her husband's safety, Kerry was setting herself up for an unhealthy dose of triangulation.

Kerry fell into the trap of seeing the hospital staff as her persecutor. Consequently, she took on the role of the victim. Kerry went to church the following Sunday and told anybody who would listen how frustrated she was with the hospital staff because they didn't seem to take her complaints seriously. By talking to anyone who would listen, Kerry was looking for a rescuer. Everybody she talked to obliged her by doing just that. Everybody agreed with her, that she was being treated poorly by the hospital staff. But none of this "rescuing" helped Kerry. The rescuing reinforced for her that she was the victim. As she continued in the role of victim Kerry continued to look for a rescuer. None of the sympathy she got gave her any help.

By trying to empathise with Kerry, and agreeing with her that the hospital staff should do something, the people Kerry shared her frustrations with were only reinforcing Kerry's idea that she was the victim of the hospital staff's persecution of her. Under normal circumstances trying to help Kerry by giving her some direction on how to approach the hospital staff with her complaint would also be of little help to her. Giving advice confirms Kerry's role as a child or victim just as much as the rescuing attempts keep her in this role.

At one point Kerry's pastor heard her complaining to another church member. He joined the conversation and when Kerry said how badly the hospital staff had treated her husband and how they were ignoring her complaints, the pastor simply said to her, "Yes, but it really upsets *you*, doesn't it?" Rather than agreeing with her, that she was a victim, the pastor focused on how it was all affecting her. She replied, "Yes" and began to cry. From that moment Kerry stopped telling anyone who would listen about her frustration with the hospital. She stopped looking for rescuers because the pastor's simple words had helped Kerry identify her real problem. She was frustrated with the hospital staff and was probably also angry with her husband because he had been drinking when he first fell. But her real issue was how it was affecting her emotionally. Because Kerry's pastor didn't play the role of rescuer but identified what was really upsetting her, she was able to move on.

In pastoral care we need to be aware of what role the person is taking on for themselves and what role they may be wanting us to play in their "drama triangle". Be aware of this and be careful you do not play an inappropriate and unhelpful role. Don't become a rescuer. A pastoral carer should never play a role in a drama triangle.

Kerry's pastor stayed out of the drama triangle because he understood the *process* that was going on in Kerry's mind. The hospital staff, while obviously unhelpful, were not persecuting her. She was not a victim, and she certainly didn't need rescuing. The pastor identified the process in the story Kerry was telling herself. She was upset by all that had happened, but she wasn't allowing herself to acknowledge this. By identifying her own pain, the pastor had helped her in the process of dealing with the pressure that was on her. The important thing in understanding process is to listen to the story the person is telling to themselves. The facts of the incident are almost irrelevant. What matters in *process* is what the person believes those facts are saying about themselves.

In *The Power of TED*, first published in 2009, David Emerald recommends that the "victim" adopt the alternative role of *creator*, view the persecutor as a *challenger*, and enlist a *coach* instead of a rescuer. This approach can be beneficial because it helps the person change the narrative. Kerry approached her situation as a victim. Emerald's suggestion is that we could help Kerry to view herself as a creator rather than a victim. In such a scenario we would participate in the drama triangle by taking on the role, not of the rescuer that Kerry is seeking, but as the coach who helps Kerry see a way forward.

However, as I said above, the pastoral carer should never play a role in a drama triangle. Even if we change the narrative, as Emerald suggests, and we become the coach rather than the rescuer, we have still stepped into the drama triangle Kerry has created for herself. I want to suggest that in a very real sense the drama that Kerry is involved in is irrelevant to the pastoral care we can offer her. Rather than get involved in a person's situation, the pastoral carer focuses on the *process*. Before I explain more fully what that means and how to do it, let's look at another case study.

PROCESS

Bruce went to see his pastor because he and his wife were having trouble. He told the pastor his wife was spending too much money, but she ignored him and continued to spend more than they could afford. The pastor, remembering something about "empathy" from his pastoral care training at seminary, said to Bruce, "She should not ignore you." Such a response seems like the pastor is showing empathy with Bruce but if you have been paying attention to what I have said above you can see clearly that the pastor has entered the drama triangle and taken on the role of rescuer. This will not help Bruce. It is not what is meant by "empathy".

What has happened in this little illustration is that Bruce went to his pastor as the victim. He saw his wife as the persecutor. This is subconscious. He doesn't think his wife is actually persecuting him, but in his frustration that she continues to spend too much money, his wife plays the role of persecutor in this triangulation. Bruce is looking to his pastor for help or advice. However, in the pastor's attempt to empathise with him the pastor has played the role of rescuer. By saying, "She should not ignore you," he has agreed with Bruce that he is the victim. What the pastor has done is kept Bruce in the role of victim and this is not empathy. It would have been better for the pastor not to try to rescue him but to try to empathise with Bruce's *emotion*. Focusing on the emotion of the person seeking pastoral care is the beginning of dealing with the *process* rather than the situation. True empathy focuses on what is going on for the person, in their own thinking or emotional responses. If we are going to show empathy, we must explore with the person what is going on inside them. We must explore how they are responding to the situation they are facing. We must discover the process that is going on within the person. What is it that they are telling themselves about their situation? Are they feeling like a victim? How are they responding to their situation emotionally?

EMOTION

The above two illustrations involving Kerry and Bruce, while highlighting how to avoid triangulation, more especially point to where pastoral care must have its focus. In the case of Kerry and her frustration with the hospital staff, the pastor has focused on her emotions. The pastor almost completely ignores Kerry's situation. This is because the most important thing is not external. It's not what is happening *to* Kerry. The important issue is what is happening *in* Kerry. It is about how Kerry is dealing with what is going on in her world. It is about her emotional response to her situation.

In the case of Bruce's frustration with his wife's spending, the pastor has played the role of rescuer. Bruce doesn't need rescuing. Like Kerry, Bruce needs to know that someone else understands how his situation is affecting him. When someone understands how we are feeling about our situation we know we are not alone. When we feel someone else understands, we feel empowered. Bruce needed his pastor to have a better understanding of the *process* Bruce was going through. To empathise is not to agree. Empathy has to do with understanding the process a person is going through. Empathy with Bruce does not say, "Your wife should not spend your money." Empathy would say something like, "You're really struggling personally with the way your wife is spending, aren't you Bruce." Empathy tries to identify the internal process or the story the person is telling themselves about what is happening externally.

Notice Kerry's reaction when the pastor made the observation that she was upset. She cried. All previous responses to Kerry's complaints resulted in people trying to rescue her. The real empathy of her pastor identifying that she was upset gave Kerry such relief that she cried. But it did more than that. After her pastor identified that she was upset, Kerry no longer felt the need to go about telling anyone who would listen about her very frustrating situation. Knowing she was not alone, gave her empowerment. The pastor's question has helped Kerry identify how she has been personally affected by what's been happening around her. Up to this point no one had identified what Kerry was feeling, not even Kerry herself. Once that feeling had been accurately identified, Kerry's attitude to her situation changed.

People will often tell you that what helped was, not advice, and not agreeing that these things shouldn't happen. What really helps is when someone just says, "Yes. That's how you feel, and that's OK." In effect this is what happened for Kerry when her pastor accurately identified that her situation was affecting Kerry's emotional response. Notice that he did not even identify the emotion. All it took was for him to accurately identify that Kerry was affected emotionally. In all previous encounters, Kerry's emotional response was not acknowledged.

This is what I mean by paying attention to the *process* rather than the situation. To pastorally care for Kerry in her situation, attention is not given to the events but to Kerry's response to the events. Attention is paid to what is going on for Kerry. Attention is paid to Kerry's emotions. This is the process.

In paying attention to the process, pastoral care pays attention to the person's emotions. Pastoral care is all about listening, not just listening to the story but listening for the person's emotional response to the story they are telling us. In the next section, we will talk about how to listen to a person's emotions.

IDENTIFYING EMOTION

When we listen to a person's story we can usually tell if they are angry, sad, distressed, happy or whatever the emotion might be. Sometimes it is not easy to pick up the emotion, especially when it is unacknowledged by the person sharing their story. Fortunately, we don't always need to accurately identify the emotion. This did not happen in Kerry's case. Her pastor did not identify which emotion Kerry was feeling. He simply identified the fact that the situation was affecting Kerry personally and emotionally. This was enough for Kerry to take her attention off the situation and acknowledge her internal reality, that she was upset.

When I say that the person's situation is not important, I don't mean we ignore the story a person is telling us about their situation. We listen to the story because it will lead us to the emotion.

Kerry and Bruce's situations are important to the pastoral care they need but how they are responding to the situation is their real pastoral need. So pastoral care will focus on how the situation is affecting Kerry or Bruce. In both cases they are facing an unacknowledged emotion. The pastoral task is to listen for the emotion. If the emotion is appropriately identified by the pastoral counsellor, the person being cared for is helped to see what the real issue is. The real issue is all about how they are responding to their situation.

In Kerry's case we see that in response to the pastor's question, "Yes, but it really upsets *you*, doesn't it?", she begins to cry. The question has helped Kerry to identify how she has been responding to her situation. Another human has drawn alongside her and acknowledged the situation has been affecting her emotionally. The response has been a caring one and has therefore given Kerry permission to acknowledge her emotions.

Kerry is helpless to stop her husband's drinking. She was not responsible for his broken bones. She cannot determine how the hospital staff will respond. All these incidents have added up to a strong emotional feeling of helplessness and frustration.

Notice in this case, the pastor's response simply identifies that Kerry is "upset". The pastor has not identified an emotion as such. He has not suggested she may be frustrated, feeling helpless or angry. He has simply identified that Kerry is having an emotional response to all that is happening around her husband. The fact that someone has empathised with her *emotion* has helped Kerry to acknowledge the toll these events are having on her. At the same time, for the first time, a person has not played the role of rescuer. The pastor has identified something is going on for Kerry herself, something internal. Suddenly, Kerry sees that someone has drawn alongside her and empathically identified her emotion. This assures Kerry that someone understands, and it allows her emotional release in the form of her tears.

When we feel another human being understands what we're going through we feel we are not alone in our struggles. Not being alone is very empowering. What's happening externally for Kerry, to some extent, is not important. Kerry can't change those things. But she can change the way she responds to them. When she feels empowered Kerry begins to see how she can take control of her own emotions and her response to what is going on around her.

Identifying a person's emotional response to their situation helps them process what they're going through. As we've noted, in Kerry's case, the actual emotion doesn't need to be identified, but it helps greatly. To be able to suggest to someone that they may be feeling frustrated, or devastated, or angry, or happy, or confused, or whatever the emotion is can give them great empowerment. If someone is listening to my emotions and identifies what I am feeling, I want to shout out, "Yes! Someone understands what's going on." That is empowering and it helps me to feel I can cope a little better with the issue I'm struggling with.

DISCOVERING EMOTIONAL PROCESSES

How, then, in pastoral counselling can we be sure we understand what emotional process a person is going through? The surprising answer is that we don't need to be sure. As we listen to a person's story, we may think they feel a certain emotion about their situation. We may think they feel a certain way because that's the way we would feel if we were in that situation. We need to understand that all people do not respond emotionally in the same way to the same situation. We respond differently depending on our upbringing or the circumstances we are currently in, which may be very different from another person's upbringing or their circumstances. We have to be careful not to impose our feelings onto the person we are trying to pastorally care for.

If we feel, and I literally mean that, *feel*, the person we're caring for has a particular emotional response to their situation, the thing to do is to check with them. We don't tell them what their emotion is. We don't say, "Oh boy! You were really anxious." Rather, we can ask them, "When that happened, were you anxious?" Or we could make a statement that shows we are a bit more confident in our understanding but still not telling the person how they felt. We could say something like, "When that happened it sounded like you were quite anxious." If we get it right, the person will feel a bit more empowered. If we get it right, we will notice the person answers with some increased energy. I have even had people shout, "Yes! That's exactly how I felt."

If we get it wrong, there's no need for panic. They are more than likely to correct us. Raising the fact that they have had an emotional response gives them the opportunity to think about what their emotion has been. If it was not the emotion you have suggested, more often than not, they will respond with something like, "No, I wasn't anxious. I was more frustrated (or whatever they have actually felt)." This is empowering for the person we're ministering to because it has given them the opportunity to reflect on their emotional response to their situation. We may have got it wrong but as they have thought about their emotional response, they have been able to identify what is really going on for them.

BEING AWARE OF OUR OWN EMOTIONS

To be able to be more confident about identifying feelings or emotions in others we need to be aware of our own emotions and feelings. This is what I mean by *feeling* the other person's emotions. If you've had any sort of counsellor training, you will be familiar with the term *projection*. Projection is when we project onto another person our own feelings. Projection is an inevitable consequence of human interaction. For example, if a friend tells you about a wonderful time they have had on their recent holiday and they communicate what a joy it has been, you will inevitably share their joy. You will actually feel joyful and happy yourself. You will move on from that conversation with your friend feeling happy. They have projected onto you the happiness they have felt from a wonderful holiday.

Any one of the people Kerry tried to recruit as a rescuer may have been able to identify her emotion. It was clear Kerry was feeling frustrated. I'm sure those she recruited as her rescuers felt her frustration as well but rather than empathise in a real way, they expressed their frustration (projected onto them from Kerry) in the same way Kerry was trying to deal with it by playing the role of victim. They were trying to deal with the situation rather than be involved with the process. Any one of them who *felt* Kerry's frustration could have helped process what was really going on by suggesting to Kerry something like, "It sounds very frustrating for you."

In pastoral counselling we remain aware of what we are feeling as we speak with someone. The emotions we are feeling may well be being projected onto us by the other person. They therefore alert us to the process the person is going through as they try to deal with what is happening around them. However, great care is needed. While the emotion we are feeling may be a projection from the other person, it may in fact not come from them at all. As we listen to a person's story, issues in our own background may be raised. We might have had a similar experience and listening to another person's story has tapped into our own past experience and we have felt some of the emotion of *our* experience rather than theirs. Discernment is needed.

In one-on-one pastoral counselling situations, we need to be attuned to our emotions. What we are feeling may be projected onto us from the other person, or it may be our own baggage, raised for us by the conversation. To discern which it might be we need to firstly acknowledge the emotion we have felt and then ask the question of ourselves, "Where's that coming from? Is it my stuff, or is it what the other person is feeling?" If we're fairly confident it is what the other person is feeling, we then check in with them, "When you described what happened, you sounded a bit …"

Pastoral care is all about listening. From the examples above you can see that we listen to the other person but at the same time we listen to our own emotions. We listen to the other person's story, hearing about actual events, but listening for how the person is responding emotionally to those events. We are listening for the process that is happening for them around the events they are describing. At the same time, we are listening to our own emotional response to the events the person is describing. When we are listening to our own emotions we are constantly checking to see if the emotion we are feeling is projected onto us from the other person, and therefore it is their emotion we are feeling, or if it is our own emotional response to what we're hearing. Is it our baggage raising its ugly head?

If it is our baggage, this is something we will need to deal with later on in our own pastoral supervision. Pastoral supervision is simply about meeting on a regular basis with a pastoral supervisor who can help us to look at our ministry more objectively. It is an essential tool for any pastor. It has a lot of benefits. Have a look back at Chapter Two for a discussion on pastoral supervision. At this point we need to keep thinking about listening.

LISTENING TO GOD

We have already noted that pastoral counselling is all about listening. Listening to the other and listening to self. But in Christian pastoral counselling there is a third person in the pastoral conversation we must listen to. In her book *Pray without Ceasing - Revitalising Pastoral Care*, Deborah van Deusen Hunsinger[25] speaks of three-dimensional listening. We listen to God, to the other and to self. This triple listening is essential in pastoral counselling. It begins with prayer, listens to the other and to self and comes back to God in prayer. For Christian pastoral care there are always three persons present in the pastoral conversation, God, ourselves and the other. We listen to all three to engage in meaningful pastoral care.

In saying that we listen to God, I am not suggesting necessarily we wait for a word of knowledge. Listening to God is simply an acknowledgment that God is present in our conversation. We therefore begin the conversation with prayer. This may be a spoken prayer with the other person,

---

25 Deborah van Deusen Hunsinger. *Pray without Ceasing - Revitalising Pastoral Care*, Eerdmans, Grand Rapids, 2006

or it may be a silent prayer where we simply ask God to be present, to help us be attentive, both to His leading and to the emotion of the other. We will ask for wisdom, discernment and understanding in this pastoral conversation. We will continue our prayer, silently, as we listen to the other. I have found on occasion that the story I am listening to raises issues I find difficult. I will pray that the Lord will help me with these and enable me to keep listening to the other and to not be distracted by the difficult issue. I will also note that these issues may be something I need to take to supervision.

I will also finish the pastoral conversation with prayer. Again, this will either be spoken or silent, or, more often my own practice is to pray after the session has finished and I take some time to reflect on what happened during the pastoral conversation. I will seek the Lord's guidance on how to continue pastoral care of the person I've been speaking with. I will also ask the Lord to be doing His work in the person for their flourishing.

MINISTERING TO THE SICK

A lot of pastoral counselling or pastoral care in a crisis situation will involve ministry to the sick. The saints expect their minister to visit the sick. It is a vital ministry of the cure of souls. We are encouraged by James that when we are sick, we should call the elders of the church (James 5:14 – 16). They should pray for the sick person and anoint them with oil in the name of Jesus. James gives us a great confidence in praying for the sick. In v.15 he tells us, "And the prayer of faith will save the one who is sick." In the 21st century we do not do this to the exclusion of modern medicine, but it seems too often we do the opposite. We call the doctor and forget to call the elders. Pastor theologians should be teaching the people of God to understand that sickness is evidence of a creation groaning in travail. The prayer of faith is a confidence that the creation will be set free from its bondage to corruption and obtain the freedom of the glory of the children of God (see Romans 8:19 – 22). This is why James is so confident that the prayer of faith will save the sick person. James is confident that the creation will be set free from its bondage to corruption. He therefore knows that prayer for the sick will have this ultimate end.

When James encourages the elders to not only pray but to also anoint with oil, he is joining in an ancient tradition, both in the Old and New Testaments, where the action of anointing with oil is a symbol of dedication to God and His service. In other words, James recognises that sickness will bring glory to God. Its symbolism is both a recognition that sickness has entered the world because of one man's sin and also that sickness is therefore a punishment as a consequence of that sin. I am not saying that God punishes us with sickness because of a sin we have committed, although that can sometimes be the case (see 1 Corinthians 11:29 – 30). What I am saying is that sickness is evidence we live in a fallen world which is under God's punishment because of Adam's sin.

If sickness is evidence of life in a fallen world and it can be direct punishment for particular sin, it is imperative that we therefore confess our sins to one another (James 5:16). This distinctive Christian attitude to sickness is something pastor teachers must take with them when they visit the sick. Of course, it would be a good idea to make sure you have been teaching God's people this attitude before you visit the sick bed. If the sick person gets the idea you are saying they are sick because God is punishing them for a particular sin, you will probably have a lot of pastoral back peddling to do.

My point is that pastoral care of the sick involves more than praying for their healing. With the sick I usually always pray for healing. But I also pray that the sick person will know *how* God is with them in their sickness. Sickness is also an opportunity to examine ourselves and to see what sin lies in us and to confess that sin. Jesus taught that natural disasters are evidence we live in a broken world. Bad things happen to good people. The Galileans whom Pilate murdered, or the people on whom the tower in Siloam fell (see Luke 13:1 – 5) were not worse sinners than anyone else. But Jesus makes the point that these two disasters serve as a warning to us that we should repent of our sins unless we die in the same way. When we see natural disasters or hear of people dying suddenly and unprepared these things serve as a warning to us that we should examine ourselves to see what sin is in us that we need to repent of.

A Christian attitude towards sickness does the same thing. Sickness alerts us to sin. It encourages us to pray that we will be saved. It encourages us to confess sin and to look for God's blessing. When I was a hospital chaplain, on one occasion when I was called to ICU, there was a middle-aged woman standing beside the bed of her dying husband. I prayed that God would have mercy on him, forgive him his sins, and receive him into heaven. I prayed for the wife that she would know God's comfort. When I looked up from my prayer, the woman was looking directly at me and said, "He had no sin." While this was the expression of love from a wife who had lived with a loving husband for more than 20 years it also did not deal with the reality of a world in rebellion against God. At that point it was not the time to teach the woman about original sin, God's justice, and our need for repentance. That was the time to rejoice with her in the loving relationship she had had with her husband and the blessing from

God this relationship had been. It was also the time to grieve with her that that loving relationship was now coming to an end. It was the time just to be with her to communicate that God also wants to be with her and her husband, or, rather, that He wants them to be with Him.

The Order for the Visitation of the Sick in the Anglican Book of Common Prayer is worth reading in full. It pulls no punches. It looks at sickness as God's "fatherly correction" and in prayer for the sick person asks that, "the sense of his weakness may add strength to his faith, and the seriousness of his repentance." This spiritual dimension of the human condition is usually missing from pastoral care of the sick in Western society. Is this because our reliance on modern medicine has led us away from reliance on God? Has this reliance on science blinded us to the reality of sin and judgement?

Pastor teachers should not be afraid to talk about sin and repentance when dealing with sickness. But if you are demonstrating real pastoral care for the flock of God you will not begin that teaching when you first visit the sick bed. Your pastoral teaching will begin a whole lot earlier. It will form part of your whole-of-life pastoral care of God's people. If you are pastorally caring for them in the whole-of-life it is they who, when they get sick, will start examining themselves to see if there is any sin in them they need to repent of, long before you get to your pastoral visit of them.

CONCLUSION

This chapter has been about pastoral counselling. It has given you some techniques to pastorally listen. It has covered how to avoid getting involved in triangulation. It has taught you how to listen to the other by listening for their emotional response to the process that goes on within them which they use to help them deal with what is happening around them. You have learned how to listen to self, to check your emotions to see if they are a projection of the person you're listening to, or if they are your own baggage raising its ugly head. You have learned to listen to God for discernment, wisdom and direction as you seek to pastorally care for one of His flock.

In this chapter I have also encouraged you to be decidedly Christian in your pastoral care. There is a spiritual dimension to crisis situations the world knows nothing about. They are an opportunity to examine ourselves to see what sin is within us. Helping people to acknowledge sin is a vital role the pastor teacher has. Leading them to repentance and faith is an essential aspect of pastoral care.

In the next chapter we will look at the difficult issue of pastoral discipline.

7

PASTORAL DISCIPLINE

CALLING OUT UNGODLY BEHAVIOUR

What place does discipline have in pastoral care? The apostle Paul was not shy about calling out ungodly behaviour. He calls the Christians in Galatia "stupid" (Galatians 3:1 NEB) because they have submitted themselves to law keeping. He tells the Christians in Corinth he does not commend them for their behaviour when they celebrate the Lord's Supper (1 Corinthians 11:17 – 22). Paul instructs Timothy to reprove, rebuke, and exhort (2 Timothy 4:2). He tells Titus to "rebuke sharply" (see Titus 1:10 – 14 ESV).

An old pastor, under whom I served when I was a student in seminary and who has since gone to glory, told me of an incident when he was a young pastor where he rebuked a man sharply. He had heard that this man was physically abusing his wife. He was so incensed at such behaviour he went around to their home, summoned the man to the front doorstep and said to him that if he wanted to hit anyone, then hit him. The pastor was up for a fight. If the man wanted one, then come out and be a man and fight a man. But leave your wife alone.

While I want to cheer my former pastor's bold approach, such a style of pastoral ministry is probably not to be recommended. But it is certainly understandable, and we all face situations where our anger is so stirred by ungodly behaviour that such a response comes easily to mind. Especially where vulnerable people are being abused. Sin in any form is not acceptable and should not be condoned. But in rebuking sin we must remember that we too are sinners. None of us can claim the higher ground. I cannot claim that my sin is not as bad as your sin. If we break one commandment, we are guilty of breaking the whole lot (see James 2:10).

SHARPLY REBUKE

How then does a pastor teacher who, like the rest of us, is a sinner, "sharply rebuke" sinful behaviour? The answer is partly in 2 Timothy 4:2 which I have quoted above. Paul tells Timothy to reprove, rebuke, and exhort but to do it with "complete patience and teaching." We don't often associate the words "rebuke" and "patience". It is hard to imagine a "sharp rebuke" (Titus 1:13) given with "complete patience". These are the pastoral skills the pastor teacher must develop.

Let's take a closer look at the words, "sharp rebuke". They are a bit more nuanced in Greek than they are in English. The first occurrence of the word "rebuke" (ἐλέγχω) in the New Testament is in Matthew 18:15, "if your brother sins against you, go to him and tell him his fault (ἐλέγχω)." The idea is that your brother has somehow "opposed" or rebuked you. The second occurrence is in Luke 3:19 which tells us about John the

Baptist's rebuke of Herod. The third occurrence is in John 3:20 where those who hate the light do not come to the light for fear of being exposed (ἐλέγχω). The fourth use of ἐλέγχω is in John 8:46 where Jesus challenges the Jews who had believed in him (John 8:31) to convict (ἐλέγχω) him of sin. The fifth, and perhaps the most surprising use of ἐλέγχω, is in John 16:8 where we are told that it is the work of the Holy Spirit to convict (ἐλέγχω) the world of sin, righteousness and judgement. Further occurrences of ἐλέγχω in the New Testament are variously translated as, "convict", "expose", "rebuke" and "reprove."

When the apostle Paul encourages Timothy and Titus to "rebuke" a person, there is no idea of verbal or physical violence. The idea is that sinful behaviour will be exposed, brought into the light and in this sense the person will be convicted and their sinful behaviour rebuked.

In Titus 1:13 where Paul tells Titus to "sharply rebuke", the idea is that the rebuke (ἐλέγχω) will be done decisively and quickly. There will be no beating around the bush. The issue of the sinful behaviour will be addressed directly and definitively with no delay. When Paul says in 2 Timothy 4:2 to rebuke, "with complete patience," he does not contradict himself. Paul is aware of the sovereignty of God and while he directs Titus to "sharply rebuke", Titus must also know that he exercises this ministry of rebuke under the sovereign hand of God and not in his own (impatient) strength.

You will notice that to the "complete patience" which Paul urges Timothy to exercise he adds, "and teaching". Here Paul connects with the role of the pastor teacher from Ephesians 4:11. The pastor pastors by teaching. The pastor rebukes by teaching. Pastoral teaching is not an academic exercise. It is done with complete patience even in situations where we might feel very angry or disgusted with the behaviour of the saint we are rebuking. While pastoral discipline is done with complete patience it can reach a point where a person must be removed from among God's people (See 1 Corinthians 5:2).

In 1 Corinthians 5 Paul addresses a very serious pastoral issue of sexual immorality. The sexual behaviour of one man is of such a distorted nature that not even pagans tolerate such behaviour. Not only is a man sexually involved with his father's wife, but the church is arrogant and boasting about it. Paul's instruction is to, "Let him who has done this be removed from among you." By this instruction Paul doesn't seem to be following his own advice to Timothy, does he? He told Timothy to, "rebuke with all patience" (2 Timothy 4:2). But in his instructions to the Christians in Corinth Paul simply says this particular sinner should be excommunicated.

Paul hardly seems to be patient with the man involved sexually with his father's wife. He gives the church instructions for a formal excommunication. He does not mean that the man should just be told to leave. Paul wants the Corinthians to formally, in a very clearly spiritual way, declare that this man's behaviour, and the arrogance of the church towards it, is unacceptable. The man is to be "handed over to Satan" (1 Corinthians 5:5). This is very serious business. But this is not an instruction to just toss him out and let Satan deal with him. The church is to assemble (v. 4). The assembly is to be in the name of Jesus and the community is to be aware that this solemn assembly is under the authority and direction of the apostle who is spiritually present in the power of our Lord Jesus (v. 4).

When the church in Corinth is gathered for this solemn assembly, they are to hand the man over "to Satan for the destruction of the flesh" (v.

5 ESV). I don't think Paul has in mind the man's death but rather the destruction of the sinful behaviour he has committed in "the flesh". There is a purpose for destroying his immoral behaviour, and that is so that his spirit may be saved in the day of the Lord (v. 5 ESV). This is the nature of sin. When it is not dealt with there is no salvation in the day of the Lord.

Our salvation is by grace through faith alone. We are saved by the work of Christ who became sin for us that we might become the righteousness of God. Salvation is not by works. We have no boasting in our own righteousness. That does not mean we can go on sinning because we have become the righteousness of God through the death of Christ. Sin such that even the pagans are amazed is not something to boast about. No sin is something to boast about. If we have been saved by grace through faith alone the proper response is to flee from sin, not boast in it. We are called upon to live out our union with Christ. As Paul will instruct later in 1 Corinthians 6, if we are united with Christ, we cannot join ourselves to a prostitute. We are joined to Christ. How can we then join ourselves to sin?

There are quite a few issues the apostle Paul addresses in 1 Corinthians. In chapter 3 he has addressed their disunity which indicates their lack of spiritual maturity (3:1 – 4). In chapter 5 he addresses incredible immoral behaviour. In chapter 6 he addresses the issue of Christians taking each other to court (vv. 6 – 11) followed by further immoral behaviour with prostitutes (vv. 12 – 20). Maybe, with so many, and so serious issues to deal with, Paul is showing a great deal of patience.

How the apostle has addressed the situation of the man sexually involved with his father's wife is instructional as to how to pastorally address sinful behaviour in members of the church. Very clearly, Paul sees this as a spiritual matter and his instructions on how to deal with this serious sin focus on the spiritual nature of the situation. The church is to assemble. Paul gives this instruction, not because every matter of sin in the congregation requires a church meeting. This assembly is necessary because the whole church has been involved in this man's sin. The congregation has been arrogant about this man's behaviour. They knew about it and seemed to have had some pride in it. Paul has said, rather than pride, they should be mourning. The whole congregation's understanding of the grace of God is so twisted that they must all come together to deal with this situation. The issue for a pastor teacher to note here is that sin is dealt with spiritually.[26]

When the Corinthians were gathered to deal with this outrageous sin, they were to recognise their gathering was in the name and power of the Lord Jesus. Sin can only be dealt with in the Lord Jesus. This sin was laid on Him (Isaiah 53:6). It is now time to come to Him in penitence and faith to acknowledge before the Lord Jesus that He became sin to deal with this very behaviour (2 Corinthians 5:21). It is to acknowledge that by continuing in this sinful behaviour we are continuing to lay this sin on Christ, and we are not becoming the righteousness of God (see 2 Corinthians 5:21).

Paul could not be at this gathering in Corinth. He at least considered its seriousness so important that it could not be delayed until he could be present sometime in the future. And so, the Corinthians are to

---

26   Understand here I am speaking about pastoral care. Where any behaviour is criminal in nature it must be referred to the police. Pastoral care does not help a person avoid the consequences of their sin. Good pastoral care will help the person understand this is the right course of action and the pastor will continue to support them through any subsequent legal process.

acknowledge that this meeting has been called by their founding pastor and apostle. In a very real sense Paul is with them in this gathering. His spiritual presence is to be acknowledged. This encourages the church to understand the seriousness of the issue being dealt with.

It is a very rare occasion that will require the whole congregation to be gathered together to deal with one person's sin. But on this occasion, of the man sexually involved with his father's wife, the whole congregation was also guilty. The church had taken pride in this man's sinful behaviour. This wrongheaded attitude of the church also needed dealing with. It was clear the Corinthians had a very flawed understanding of the fundamental nature of grace. Grace does not permit ongoing sin. Grace rebukes sin and very patiently draws us back to a life that reflects the relationship we have with Christ. The goal of pastoral discipline is always forgiveness and restoration.

GO TO HIM

Jesus said, "If your brother offends you, go to him."

More often than not where sinful behaviour needs to be confronted by the pastor teacher the best approach is that taught by Jesus in Matthew 18:15 – 20. While this teaching is about personal sin against yourself, it does give some effective instructions about how to deal with sin in the Christian community. Jesus' instruction is firstly to treat the matter privately. If it is not a public issue, and doesn't need to be one, keep it private. If the pastor teacher can approach a member of the congregation about sinful behaviour they should firstly do this without getting others involved. If the person listens, is convicted and repents of their sin, as Jesus says, "you have won your brother."

Here is a real-life example of pastoral discipline. Jim had accepted the invitation to a new parish and was greatly encouraged by the warm welcome and the desire of the leaders of the church to see him develop a faithful biblical ministry. He was particularly pleased with the ministry of his Rector's Warden, Jane, and her care of him and his family as they settled in. He relied on Jane's advice, which she gave freely, to help him understand how things had been done in the past in his new context. The trouble was that as Jim relied on this advice, he soon discovered that what Jane was telling him about "the way we have done things in the past" was not at all the way things had been done but were her own personal preferences for the way she wanted things done. What Jane was telling Jim were in fact new things that had never been done in this church before. Added to this, when Jim asked Jane if she had completed important tasks he had asked her to do, she responded that, yes indeed, they had been completed. Jim initially was very relieved to think he had a warden who was so reliable. Unfortunately, he soon discovered her lies.

Lying is a particularly destructive sin. You can't build relationships on lies. You can't work with someone who lies because their lies indicate their unreliability. Jim had a difficult task on his hands. His warden had been very helpful and kind, but her lying had to be addressed. His initial thinking was that Jane should step down from her role of leadership in the congregation, but he worried about what implications this may have in the rest of the church. He was not confident that he yet understood the personal dynamics in the church and what repercussions Jane's sacking might have. Would the latter state be worse than the former?

Jim asked Jane to come to his office. He made it clear he had an issue of concern he needed to discuss with her which involved her reliability. He asked Jane about one particularly important task she said she had completed but in fact had not done so. Jane's response was that she had meant to complete the task but had forgotten about it. Jim reminded her that when he had asked if she had done what he had asked, she had told him, yes, the task had been completed. Jim added that this had meant Jane had not told him the truth and therefore it put a strain on their relationship. Jim could not rely on Jane if she was not completely honest with him. Jane's response to Jim's explanation of why her lie was a serious breach of trust was to simply repeat that she had meant to do it but had forgotten. Jane either was minimising her sinful behaviour or she genuinely couldn't see that telling someone you had completed a task when in fact you only had the intention of doing it, was actual lying.

Jim had two options. If Jane was truly aware she had lied and was trying to minimise this behaviour because she was ashamed of it, Jim had some pastoral counselling to do with Jane. If Jane was genuinely not aware that she had lied, she probably was exhibiting some deeper psychological issues which it would probably be best for a professional psychologist or counsellor to deal with. Either way, until it was sorted out, Jim believed he had to ask Jane to step aside from her ministry of Rector's Warden. He could not work with her if he did not have confidence she would tell him the truth.

These are the sorts of issues pastor teachers deal with as they work hard at equipping the saints for the work of ministry. Hard decisions have to be made, especially when dealing with sinful behaviour. They are made in the context and with the humility of realising that, I too, am a sinner. Pastoral care is never exercised with an attitude of, "I am better than you." Jim could certainly not say to Jane that he never tells lies. The "white" lies he has told to avoid embarrassment were speaking too loudly to his own conscience. Pastoral care is one rescued sinner saying to another rescued sinner, "Stay with Jesus and live a life that shows you love him."

If Jim decides Jane needs professional counselling, he will be recognising he is not qualified to give Jane this extra help. But in referring Jane for counselling Jim will not abdicate his responsibility of pastoral care of Jane. He will maintain relationship with her, checking in on how the counselling is going. In doing this he will not cross professional boundaries. He will realise that Jane might face same personal issues in counselling she is not yet prepared or able to share with her pastor. As her pastor, Jim will respect these sorts of boundaries while making it clear that he is there for Jane to support her through the process in whatever way is appropriate. Clearly, these are not easy issues to decide how much or how little to be involved in but that is the task of the pastor teacher. Great wisdom and discernment are needed in ministry.

When confronting sinful behaviour, pastor teachers will often have the task of helping their people to understand what they have done is in fact sinful. The simple test for human behaviour is what God says about it. Most of our sinful behaviour is so clearly against how God tells us to behave it is easy to see. In Jane's case it was a simple breach of God's desire for truth (see Exodus 20:16, Leviticus 6:3, Joshua 7:11, Psalm 78:36, Isaiah 57:11, Acts 5:4, John 4:23). While helping people to acknowledge their sinful behaviour pastor teachers will also be encouraging them to know that there is real forgiveness for sin.

UNDERSTANDING FORGIVENESS

Some people find the idea of forgiveness is hard to accept. When I was a prison chaplain, I had a number of men tell me they understood the

Bible's teaching about forgiveness. Often, they would speak about the thief on the cross and understand how Jesus can forgive anyone, "even a criminal like me." But they would then add, "But I can't forgive myself." Such thinking is often the real barrier to truly understanding the forgiveness that Christ brings.

Sometimes we cannot forgive ourselves because the embarrassment of what we have done remains with us. Our sinful actions can have adversely affected others, and we cannot undo their pain caused by our behaviour. This type of situation is sometimes dealt within the criminal justice system by a process of restorative justice. Restorative justice brings the perpetrator and the victim together. The victim is given opportunity to say how the crime has hurt them and affected their lives. This is very powerful because most criminals have no concept that their crime actually hurts anyone. When the criminal hears and understands their crime has damaged a fellow human being, their sense of guilt can be palpable. After the victim has spoken, the criminal is given the opportunity to speak. If they have been touched by the personal impact of their crime on the other person (and they often are), they are often able to give a heartfelt and emotional apology.

Restorative justice is a very emotional experience. It can only happen where both parties desire to meet and express their emotions. They come into the process with some understanding that it will be very difficult. But that's what dealing with sin is. It's difficult. To know God's forgiveness, we have to willingly enter a difficult process of coming together to understand the terrible cost of sin. The sinner and the victim, who is Christ, come together to listen and to understand.

We sometimes have difficulty in understanding forgiveness because we tend to think forgiveness means everything is O.K. We think forgiveness means the crime, or the sin, doesn't matter. But that is not what forgiveness means. In understanding that we are completely forgiven in Christ, we are not to think that what we did in our sinful behaviour was therefore somehow O.K. Sin is never O.K. Sin is a distrust of God. This is highlighted in the Garden of Eden when doubt was put into the minds of Adam and Eve that God was trustworthy. God said, "Don't eat this fruit. If you eat it, you will die." That's a really easy commandment to follow. Especially when the garden is filled with every other tree, bearing all kinds of fruits. Why, on earth, would you want to eat that one fruit God has told you not to eat, when there is so much rich choice in the rest of the garden? Well, you make the decision to eat that one fruit when doubt is placed in your mind that God is trustworthy. Taking and eating that one fruit is a clear statement of unbelief in God's trustworthiness.

Understanding forgiveness is understanding that God is trustworthy. It is understanding that, while my sinful behaviour has demonstrated a lack of trust in God, God has still come back at me with His love in His Son. I sit with God and hear Him tell me about His pain caused by my sinful behaviour and I am moved to ask for forgiveness. I am still left with the memory of my sin, but Jesus and I have come together in a process of restorative justice. We acknowledge the cost of my sin, and we move forward together. I am so astounded by His love and forgiveness I am resolved to live in a way that honours him and demonstrates my trust in him.

Not being able to forgive yourself can often mean a lack of understanding of the nature of guilt. Understanding the biblical concept of guilt can be difficult when we live in a shame culture. In the West we talk a lot about shame. We talk about "naming and shaming" people or corporations who, according to general consensus, have done something wrong and seem to be getting away with it. We talk about the shame bad behaviour brings upon one's family. A Christian friend of mine who had been discovered to have been involved in an extra-marital affair over many years, told me she felt so ashamed of what she had done. But shame and guilt are two very different things. Shame is more about the embarrassment we have caused ourselves and others. Shame is not concerned with the sin but only with the consequences of the sin. Guilt is knowing we have offended a holy God. It is recognising the distrust we have of God expressed by the offence. Guilt also then understands the impact our sin has had on us and others.

When I read Psalm 51, I am initially a little disturbed by David's confession of his sin of rape of Bathsheba and the murder of her husband Uriah. David says to God, "Against you, you only have I sinned" (Psalm 51:4). I find I am angry at David. Has he minimised the impact of his lust? Does he not understand the shame Bathsheba must have felt, not being able to refuse her king's sexual advances while her own husband was away at war? Does he not have any compassion for Uriah whom he murdered to cover up his despicable behaviour?

If David had felt ashamed (rather than guilty) of his sin when confronted about it by the prophet Nathan (see the title of Psalm 51 and 2 Samuel 12:1 – 14), I think we would see in his confession some acknowledgement of the pain he has caused Bathsheba and his disgraceful manipulations to achieve Uriah's murder. But forgiveness does not come through shame. Forgiveness comes from God. Dealing with sin, even sin that has caused others great loss, is acknowledging that guilt lies in my behaviour which has demonstrated a lack of trust in God. The great loss caused to others by sin finds its zenith in the deterioration of the image of God in that person. By treating Bathsheba as an object of lust David has lessened the image of God in her. Her flourishing in life to bring glory to God as His image has been abused and diminished. David has sinned against God because his sin has resulted in less glory being ascribed to God by the abuse of an image of God.

David's prayer of confession in Psalm 51 acknowledges his sin is first and foremost an exhibition of distrust of God. Where God has made it abundantly clear that we are not to commit adultery, David has said, "No, Lord. I trust my sexual desires more than I trust you. Giving in to my lust will give me more immediate pleasure than you will, Lord." God has also made it very clear that we are not to commit murder, but David has said, "No, Lord. I can't trust you to make my sin right. I have to cover up my adultery myself by getting rid of the husband."

Put in these terms, you can see how, when finally confronted with his sin, David turns to the Lord for forgiveness. His behaviour has demonstrated an abject failure to trust God and an abuse of God's image resulting in less glory being ascribed to God. And so, with his acts of rape and murder in mind, David turns to God, whom he has offended, for forgiveness. In fact, by acknowledging that it is against God only that he has sinned, David has done so much more than just feel shame for his sin against Uriah and Bathsheba. By seeking God's forgiveness, David has realised the reason God has told us not to commit adultery and murder is because these behaviours adversely affect all those involved. By acknowledging his distrust of God by breaking these two commandments, David also acknowledges the impact his sin has had on his victims.

To understand the nature of God's forgiveness, and therefore to forgive ourselves, is to understand that all sin is distrust of God. Forgiveness is not about dealing with shame. Forgiveness is understanding God is trustworthy. Forgiveness is knowing our guilt has been laid on Christ and dealt with. Forgiveness does not ignore the impact our sin has had on us and on others. Acknowledging our guilt recognises what we have done to others expresses our distrust of God.

The apostle Paul says, "godly grief produces a repentance that leads to salvation without regret, whereas worldly grief produces death" (2 Corinthians 7:10. ESV). Paul distinguishes "godly grief" and "worldly grief". Godly grief produces a repentance that leads to salvation without regret. Godly grief recognises our offence against God. It will produce repentance in us, leading us to ask God for His forgiveness. Trusting God for His forgiveness ensures us of salvation. Knowing therefore that our sin is forgiven, we will have no regrets, no long-lasting shame. On the other hand, worldly grief simply produces death. My friend, who was discovered to have been in a long-term adulterous relationship, could not deal with the shame she felt. She went into a spiral of depression, with long stays in hospital until she finally took her own life. Her grief was worldly. She remained ashamed and never came to understand godly grief.

Understanding forgiveness is a deeply spiritual process. As the apostle Paul called the congregation at Corinth together to deal with the sin of the man involved sexually with his father's wife, so we bring our own sin before God. We sit with God in a prayerful session of restorative justice. We listen. Our sin has sent Jesus to the cross and so we listen to Christ's impact statement. We will read what the Scriptures say about our sin and as we listen, we will be confronted by how much our behaviour has caused Christ's pain and the pain of any other human victims. Being so confronted, we will seek God's forgiveness, for it is against him, him only that we have demonstrated our lack of trust.

ACCOUNTABILITY

There are times, when dealing with sin in the congregation it is appropriate to set up some process of accountability. Supportive, balanced relationships are necessary for accountability. Where we have trusting, non-judgemental relationships with God's people we develop patterns of honesty and accountability. We develop community where we are supported and strengthened to follow a biblical ethic. In such a supportive community, in the body of Christ, we speak the truth in love and grow into Christ (Ephesians 4:15). Speaking the truth in love is being accountable to each other in the church. Developing such a community is the business of whole-of-life pastoral care. If we don't have this sort of community other forms and programs of accountability will struggle. The basis for accountability needs to be set in supportive relationships in the body of Christ before programs.

Some churches seek to help men avoid the online temptations of pornography by installing software on their computers that monitors which internet sites they visit and sends a report to an accountability partner. This can be effective, but it is not infallible. To be of the greatest help men need to see they are part of Christ's community and feel that members of this community love to maintain a standard of behaviour that honours Christ. Helping to develop this community, where God's people value its high standard of Christian principles, is pastoral care.

Another form of accountability I have seen to be very effective is something that was developed in North America to help sex offenders re-adjust to life when re-entering the community after their prison sentence. It is called Circles of Accountability. In the criminal justice system this program has had a high level of success in reducing the rate of recidivism not only for sex offenders but also in helping other criminals break the cycle of offending.

In a circle of accountability, a group is assigned to "encircle" the offender so that he or she has people they will be accountable to. The group meets regularly to check in and to give support and encouragement. Members are also on call so that the person being cared for can call them for support when they are struggling. I have found this type of accountability very real when a member of the congregation has been found to have been involved in sexual sin.

When anyone in Christ's church needs support because of sin we must be careful to ensure the support is offered in a non-judgemental way. At the same time, we must communicate that sin is not O.K. Balance is needed.

Some years ago, I was a member of a church that took its responsibility to its youth seriously. The elders recognised the temptations of youth to sexual sin and decided to institute a regular program of sex education with specific teaching about how a young Christian person should deal with their sexual desires in a godly way. As part of the program, the youth had a weekend away. You can see where this is going, can't you? These weekends became known as the youth "sexathon".

With parental approval, the youth of this church were given detailed sex education. Medical experts and counsellors contributed. The pastor gave excellent Bible studies on God's desire for a people who are sexually pure. The education the youth received gave them ideas they had not had before. Some of them said, "I didn't know you could do that!" And so, they began to experiment. What had begun with good intentions of educating the youth about godly behaviour ended in giving them information that helped them experiment with immoral conduct.

Great care is needed when dealing with sin. The best pastoral care you can offer God's people is to develop Christian community which builds itself in love (Ephesians 4:16).

Understanding the nature of sin, knowing in Christ we have been forgiven and therefore are able to forgive ourselves, is a deeply spiritual process. Understanding guilt and forgiveness will often be the issue pastor teachers are called on to help God's people with. It requires great spiritual wisdom and humility from the pastor teacher to assure a parishioner that in Christ, their sin has been dealt with and is no more. This is pastoral care.

This is why the task of pastoral care remains firmly in the realm of theology and why the pastor teacher must be well trained in theology. This is why what you learn in college works in the real world. The task of pastor teachers is to encourage God's flock to continually trust God in everything they do. Pastor teachers do this, not only when people are in crisis or when pastoral discipline is needed, but all the time, in the way Sunday meetings are run and in the way they exercise their ministry to develop a whole community of God, which is the body of Christ.

CONCLUSION

The aim of this book has been to encourage those in pastoral ministry to restore pastoral care to its full function, together with the word of God, which is, to build the body of Christ by equipping the saints for the work of ministry.

When caring for the flock of Christ, pastor teachers will work to ensure their whole ministry is one of pastoral care. Whether they are writing reports for the Denominational hierarchy, or sitting with a young couple who has lost a child, pastor teachers will focus their attention on caring for God's people. The business of running a church is not the focus of pastor teachers. It is a necessary function, which sometimes can be delegated, but it is not the core of ministry. Pastor teachers can pretend they are very busy with church business, but this is not where they should be directing their attention.

I remember at a clergy conference, our Bishop told us he wanted each of us to write regular reports to him of what efforts we had made in the past month in evangelism. We were to include the results, how many people spoken to, what evangelistic events had been run, and how many people had been converted. Imagining the clergy would be spending time collecting statistics, writing reports, sending reports to our Bishop only to be filed away, I asked what was the purpose of this extra administrative burden. "For the gospel, brother. For the gospel," was the unapproachable reply. I have to tell you that such an unthought out direction from the Bishop to burden us with more administration, "for the gospel," was not my idea of gospel ministry. For the pastor teacher, ministry is the cure of souls, equipping the saints for ministry. My hope is that what you have learned from this book will encourage you to be decidedly one eyed in your approach to the cure of souls, keeping your focus in everything you do on the pastoral care of God's people.

Building the body of Christ is what the gift of Christ to His church does. That gift is apostles, prophets, evangelists, pastors and teachers. Pastors and teachers work with the Scriptures (the apostles, prophets and evangelists) to equip the saints. You can't equip the saints if you are not teaching them the Bible. Pastoral care is not just telling stories. Pastor teachers teach the word of God. Pastoral care is not taking on the activity of a counsellor or simply referring a person for counselling and forgetting about them.

The focus for pastor teachers, to ensure the saints are well taught, is both individual and corporate. On-the-run pastoral care and pastoral counselling focus on the individual. This focus is whole-of-life. It doesn't just seek to help people in crisis, although, of course, it will do this. Pastoral care also focuses on equipping Christian people to live in the world with a focus on God. Helping to create Christian community focuses on corporate pastoral care.

I say the pastor teachers' focus is to *help* create Christian community because creating Christian community is actually the role of the saints. The saints are equipped by the Scriptures and pastor teachers to build the body of Christ. The body of Christ, the local church, is Christian community. When the body is being built, it grows in love, maturity and unity. Within this body, this Christian community, God's people receive loving pastoral support.

Helping God's people to have their focus on God is the business of pastoral care. It is a spiritual activity. Western psychology has hijacked the idea of pastoral care and handed it back to Christians, unexamined and stripped of true spirituality. This is why pastor teachers must be pastor theologians. Those charged with the responsibility of caring for God's flock must think theologically, biblically, so that the focus of their ministry remains what God intended it to be. They must maintain a clear, biblical vision of what Christian ministry is and be able to theologically examine new innovations. They must be able to reject those things that water down Christ's teaching but, rejoicing in God, accept those things that will help them to be better pastor teachers.

The role of pastor teachers is not to just fill heads with biblical knowledge. Pastoral care equips God's people for ministry. Pastoral care, in this sense, has its focus on action. God's people are taught to build the body of Christ in love. They are also taught how to act *Christianly* in the world in such a way that the world sits up and takes notice. By Christians being the salt and light in the world, that Jesus said we are (Matthew 5:13 – 16), the world will understand that humanity's identity is in God, as His image, and not in *self*. This whole-of-life pastoral care is the definition of the *cure of souls*. It is the work the pastor teacher does to equip the people of God to build a sacred community, which is the body of Christ, and to live in the secular world.

Pastoral care recognises life is messy. We live in a world scarred by sin.

Pastoral ministry, while recognising sin is wrong, will draw alongside the hurting person because they are someone created in God's image. Pastoral care will offer this person non-judgemental presence, time and an ear. In this messiness of life pastoral care also recognises God's people live in the world. The world has competing ideas and philosophies among which the Christian voice is but one. Pastoral care will equip the saints to speak lovingly of God's love into this world.

The whole ministry of the ordained minister is pastoral care. Everything pastor teachers do will be directed at pastorally caring for God's flock. Pastor teachers will probably have to write some reports for the denominational hierarchy, but ask yourself if that administrative task helps you to bring pastoral care to God's people. If it does, well and good. If it doesn't, forget it. Or, at least challenge it, as you are able.

You will probably have other demands on your time that threaten to take you away from pastoral care. You are trained to think theologically. Assess everything in the light of what the Scriptures say a pastor teacher must be doing. Will the demand on your time help you to bring pastoral care to God's people? If it does, well and good. If it doesn't, forget it. Or, maybe you could delegate it.

To equip the saints to build Christ's body you will have to be in touch with the world. You will need to know what issues in the world the people in the congregation God has placed you in, are dealing with. What are the issues being spoken of and debated in the public square that the saints want to contribute a Christian perspective to? Your task as a pastor teacher is to equip the saints with a Christian mind so they have a valuable and respected contribution to make to Western secular society.

Pastoral care expresses the character of God. God is love. God expresses

His love towards us by serving us (see Mark 10:45). Pastoral care will therefore seek to serve people. In love, pastoral care does not condemn even when it rebukes sharply. Pastoral care does not shoot the wounded of God's people. The pastor teacher draws alongside with the aim of restoration. God is also Three in One. Pastoral care seeks to help God's people create a diverse community, the body of Christ, where all are welcomed as one family under God. In creating humanity, God's desire was to be in fellowship with us. Pastoral care will help the saints build the body of Christ so that we will have fellowship with each other and with the Father.

When God's people ask their pastors to get Sunday right, they are simply asking them to give them pastoral care. They are asking their pastors to equip them in their whole-of-life to build the body of Christ.

Contrary to current Western thinking about the functions of pastoral care, it is not the task of pastoral ministry to help people have a better life in this world. Pastoral care does not aim to improve people, nor does it assign economic value to them, as though we can make their life more "valuable". The aim of pastoral ministry is to encourage a person to know they are created in the image of God and that God is with them no matter what is happening around them or to them. The aim is to lift their eyes heavenward and to give the soul wings. This will happen when the saints are equipped to build the body of Christ.

Finally, pastor teachers must take care of themselves. Take your day off. Have pastoral supervision. Understand the sovereignty of God. You are convinced pastoral ministry is what God wants you to be doing. Make sure you have all the supports you need to do it well so that the body of Christ is built.

BIBLIOGRAPHY

Adams, Jay E. *Shepherding God's Flock: A Handbook on Pastoral Ministry, Counseling, and Leadership*. Grand Rapids. Zondervan. 1974 1975

Browning, Donald S. "Introduction to Pastoral Counselling" in *Clinical Handbook of Pastoral Counselling*, Volume 1, Expanded Edition, ed. Robert J. Wicks, Richard D. Parsons, Donald Capps, Mahwah, New Jersey. Paulist Press, 1985

Clinton E. Arnold. *Ephesians (Zondervan Exegetical Commentary on The New Testament series Book 10)*. Grand Rapids. Zondervan Academic. 2010.

Collier, Winn. *A Burning in My Bones – The Authorized Biography of Eugene H. Peterson*. London. Authentic. 2022.

Gibbs, Eddie, Bolger, Ryan. *Emerging Churches - creating Christian community in postmodern cultures*, SPCK. 2006.

Kuruvilla, Abraham. *A Vision for Preaching – Understanding the Heart of Pastoral Ministry*. Grand Rapids. Baker Academic. 2015.

Leins, Chris J. K. "What Makes Pastoral Counseling So Pastoral? Distinguishing Between Pastoral Care and Clinical Practice in

Modern Life," *Journal of Psychology and Christianity,* Vol. 40, No. 4 (2021)

Peterson, Eugene H. "Reforming Spiritual-Health Care" https://www.christianitytoday.com/pastors/books/counselcare/lldev03-1.html 1997. Accessed 19 July 2018

Purves, Andrew. *Pastoral Theology in the Classical Tradition.* Westminster, John Knox Press. 2005

Robinson, Marilynne. *Gilead.* London, Virago 2009

Stott, John. *The Living Church – The convictions of a lifelong pastor.* IVP, 2007, 2021

van Deusen Hunsinger, Deborah. *Pray without Ceasing – Revitalising Pastoral Care.* Grand Rapids, Eerdmans. 2006

Wengert, Timothy J. "The Priesthood of All Believers and Other Pious Myths," Institute of Liturgical Studies Occasional Papers. Paper 117 2006

Wilson, Todd and Gerald Hiestand (Eds.) *Becoming a Pastor Theologian: New Possibilities for Church Leadership.* InterVarsity Press. 2016. Kindle Edition.

www.ingramcontent.com/pod-product-compliance
Lightning Source LLC
LaVergne TN
LVHW051558070426
835507LV00021B/2636